Queenie. A novel. [By May Crommelin.]

Anonymous

Queenie. A novel. [By May Crommelin.]
Anonymous
British Library, Historical Print Editions
British Library
1874
3 vol. ; 8º.

The BiblioLife Network

GUIDE TO FOLD-OUTS, MAPS and OVERSIZED IMAGES

QUEENIE.

VOL. III.

QUEENIE.

A NOVEL.

"We sail the sea of life: a calm one finds,
And one a tempest: and, the voyage o'er,
Death is the quiet haven of us all."

WORDSWORTH.

IN THREE VOLUMES.

VOL. III.

LONDON:
HURST AND BLACKETT, PUBLISHERS,
13, GREAT MARLBOROUGH STREET.
1874.

LONDON:
PRINTED BY MACDONALD AND TUGWELL, BLENHEIM HOUSE,
BLENHEIM STREET, OXFORD STREET.

QUEENIE.

CHAPTER I.

THOSE WHOM THE GODS LOVE DIE YOUNG.

"Of all the gifts of God that are
Borne inward into souls afar,
Along the Psalmist's music deep;
Now tell me if that any is,
For gifts or grace surpassing this—
He giveth His belovëd sleep?"

IT did not last very long—only that night and part of the next day. How like a mere troubled, vivid dream the whole scene comes back, and Nellie and I are once more sitting, in the dead of night, in that darkened room, with the dim nightlight burning like an evil eye behind the screening curtains. Whispers sound occasionally from the dressing-room beyond, and the doctor or the old nurse glide in with iced cloths to place on that burning childish head; but only a faint moan sometimes breaks the lethargy in which the little figure lies. A short while ago, and he had called us in his ravings. "Queenie! Nellie! . . . Norah! Norah! That bird's nest, you know—I can't get it now. I am so tired . . . I want to go home." But no recognition in those wide blue eyes met our tearful, anxious glances, and after a time the calls became less frequent, till finally a creeping torpor, whether sleep or insensibility we could hardly tell, settled down upon him towards morning.

"Thank God for it," I murmured to myself in those cold, chilly hours of that dark December morning, when the piteous calls for those loving ones who were close beside him, the burning of that feverish little golden head, the moans of pain, had passed away into that drowsy unconsciousness.

It was almost seven, that dark morning, when our aunt and Sophia, who had left us a few hours before, stole in again, like ghostly white spirits, and motioned us to lie down awhile in our turn. Nellie was crouched upon the sofa, her head on her hand, and her eyes fixed upon that little heap in the midst of the white expanse of pillows and coverings—watching—watching—while a few moments before I had turned away mutely from the same sad sight, to look out into the wild, wet outside darkness, and pray for help and comfort, as at such times only one *does* pray, when death under our eyes shows us how near we are to that spirit-land whose view we strive to hide out at other times by our material senses. "Eat, drink, and be merry," yet "to-morrow we die." Nay, rather let us pray ever to be near Him, as at such times, "nearer to Thee, e'en though it be a cross that raiseth me."

Only for two hours Nellie and I laid ourselves down on my bed, unable to sleep, yet stupefied into semi-unconsciousness from pain and the unusual watching. The short day seemed to drag along so wearily to those watchers, waiting and hoping that some lucid moment—if but a second of awakening—should gladden them before the end, though he lay so quietly, it seemed half wrong to wish it.

At last it came! The sun was slowly sinking down in a crimson globe of fire behind a low, dark bank of clouds; its dying glow just tinged the outer branches of the old Scotch fir beside the windows—how clearly everyone of their rugged tufts and twigs stands out against the sky again as I remember it!—when he awoke.

"Our Father . . ." said the child. And as we knelt and repeated the prayer, his eyes closed again with a smile of recognition.

One moment again he opened them, while we watched him, and tremblingly held our breath.

"Mama, mama," he said gently; then clasping his little hands on his breast, seemed to smile himself asleep with a half-sigh, like a happy, tired child at rest.

Only one short sigh. . . . . .

"He has gone to her," said our aunt in awed, trembling tones, while we hushed our grief in the presence of that holy, peaceful stillness.

* * * * * *

Then came a day when we watched with

straining eyes the last glimpse of that dark procession winding towards the church under the pine-trees, and, as it turned the corner, remembering his last farewell to me on that fatal day, I too, through my thick sobs, called softly to those dull ears which should hear no more,

"Good-bye, Davie! Good-bye, my darling—it may be for many a year, but not for ever."

Then they laid dust to dust, and ashes to ashes, beyond the spruce-fir trees in the little church-yard: one more earthly flower in God's-acre down below, while the spirit was happy in that blessed Place of Souls.

"It cannot be so far away," I thought to myself, still gazing, on my knees at the window, towards the wood—"Not so very far away! '*To-day shalt thou be with me in Paradise.*'"

Sorrowfully for us came that Christmas

morning, which seemed so lonely with the circle broken; the one little, living link gone, leaving us weeping for the gap in our ring where a soft clasp had been. We were younger at our parents' death, and had joined hands again—now we were severed sharply, never to be joined in quite the same way. Has not everyone known such times of heavy sorrow, weariness of daily tasks, awe-struck faces when some trifle, toy, or careless word recalled the absence among us and the empty place. Happy those who have not yet felt a time when, for them, all the world seems darkening over; and it seems as if the sun would never shine just *so* again.

"Who that a watcher doth remain
Beside a couch of mortal pain,
Deems he can ever smile again?

. . . .

Oh, hearts of ours so weak and poor
That nothing there can long endure,
And so their hurts find shameful cure."

And so the months passed away, till March with its strong winds came to an end. The neighbours called and condoled, and thought, it may be, that we took it quietly, but people mourn differently—and we sisters always tried to restrain any outward show. "We should go to him, but he could not return to us."

Sometimes that control almost broke down the barriers, and we could have wished for anything—excitement—change—no matter what, if only something to drown for a little while that close, hushed sorrow, and silence its voice in any noise or loud whirl of forced gaiety.

Then that feeling too passed away; but our dead boy was not forgotten any the more that we seldom cared to speak of him.

CHAPTER II.

SLIGHTED LOVE IS ILL TO BIDE.

"Anfangs wollt' ich fast verzagen,
Und ich glaubt', ich trüg' es nie,
Und ich hab' es doch getragen,—
Aber fragt mich nur nicht wie?"

I WAS sitting with my sisters one March morning in the drawing-room; our usual habit after breakfast till the post came. This event never occurred till nearly eleven, or it might be much later, according to the varying sobriety, or rather inebriety, of the ancient postman, who was so often pressed by sympathising friends to take a "half-one (of whisky)," that little dependence could be placed upon his punctuality.

"Oh! the old man does well enough; he is as honest as the day, at all events," Mr. Burke, who hated change or reform in any shape, would say at such times. "He is always safe to turn up at some time or other in the day, and you ought to be very thankful to get any post at all. In my young days we only got it twice a week, and were far more happy and contented."

On this particular morning the post is even later than usual, but we have already exhausted our accustomed grumbles.

"It will be quite a new sensation having the house to myself when you two are married and done for."

"Poor Queenie! I hope you won't miss us dreadfully," answers Nellie, as she shuts her book with a stretch and a yawn, and looks at me with much commiseration.

"Well, it is strange," thoughtfully observes Sophy, with her head on one side. "If anyone had asked me which of us all was most likely to be married, I should have said it was you, Queen."

"Never mind; I am not in the slightest degree jealous of either of you two young persons," I reply. "On the whole, I may find it a great advantage to have my own way in everything. They will be much kinder to me when I am alone, that is certain, and being the only daughter of the house will be quite an agreeable novelty."

This is a piece of utter hypocrisy on my part, but I have tried to act up to it with varying success ever since last January, when one evening Sophia first told us brusquely she had engaged herself to our cousin. Yes, that dissimilar couple had found out for themselves what other eyes had seen before, and in some original fashion of their own had made the fact clear to each other. Nellie was of the opinion that the final explanation took place in a ploughed field, which the lady's obstinacy induced her to cross, and that his determination to accompany her through the wet, sticky furrows had heightened her opinion of him, and helped on the declaration; while I was equally convinced that a violent war of words on the subjects of emigration and immigration, of which I had overheard the commencement, had been twisted by the gentleman to suit ulterior purposes.

It is only certain, however, that when, in the beginning of the year, our guardian had explained to John that, owing to the different circumstances in which we were placed, they must hold a family consultation, since a large share of the property had, by Davie's death, accrued to John's father—though the house and rest of the estate devolved to Sophia—our cousin took the opportunity of hinting that the easiest way of settling matters might be for Sophia and him to "bank together," as he expressed it, and thereupon soon put his hint into execution.

His parents were delighted, and wrote warm congratulations to their daughter, as they already called her; and with a rapidity which all but took our breath away, all had been settled. Both sisters were to be married very quietly in the beginning of April; and while Nellie and her husband meant to travel about for some time, the others were bound for Canada, almost immediately after their marriage.

On one point only John showed himself inflexible, and, strangely enough, as I thought, Sophia entirely agreed with him—and this moot point was his utter refusal to live, for the present at least, at Ballymore. He had tried the old country, he told us, and liked it on the whole, still Canada could beat it into fits; so, for a year or two, at least, he wished Sophia to give his country a fair trial; whereupon, to our consternation, Sophia declared it to be her greatest wish to live in one of the colonies, saying she was convinced life would be pleasanter in a new country, where society was less exclusively stiff and reserved, and old-world prejudices and traditions had not compelled opinions and manners to abide in fixed, unalterable grooves.

"People here think more of precedence than principles," she had exclaimed. 'And the bigotry, cold narrow-mindedness, and suppression of all honest freedom and originality of thought with which she had been met on every side since her cradle, disgusted her; out there she hoped and believed that Mind would be put before Manners, while here the great ambition of her acquaintance was to push vulgarly into a circle of society above them, instead of attaining a higher level of thought and intellect.'

"Perhaps so," said I, rather practically, "but human nature, I should imagine, is pretty much the same everywhere—a few distinctions without much difference."

"At all events, Americans are free from the detestable British adoration of the peerage," she had answered, with scorn.

"And get, in exchange, the Worship of Mammon," I replied.

The knot was finally cut by the Burkes'

offer of taking Ballymore off the young people's hands for the next five years; and, as our uncle had no house of his own to which he could take Norah and me, since he and his wife had never settled down anywhere, this was perhaps the best plan, and gave me, at least, undoubted satisfaction.

So this is why we are discussing the question of my future position, in an idle after-breakfast conclave.

The letters come at last, and as Aunt Emily enters and takes up the pile addressed to herself, she carelessly says,

"A Canadian stamp! Whose writing is this, I wonder?"

Whose writing! My heart stood still for a moment, and then gave a quick, wild flutter, for I knew it even from where I sat by the window.

"Captain Graham, I declare!" she exclaimed, after a second or two; "and full of congratulations to you, Sophia. Quite a newsy epistle." And thereupon she proceeded to read it aloud, stopping, every now and then, to deliver remarks and side-references, while my sisters listened, with observations and quick expressions of friendly interest, that made me, in my impotent misery, wish myself leagues away.

After speaking of the pleasant days he had spent at Ballymore, which, together with the kindness shown him by the Demerics at Montreal, induced him to write—as he hoped to meet Sophia on her arrival; he spoke enthusiastically of the kindness our relations had shown him on Mrs. Burke's introduction.

"Why, he seems to be there perpetually," observed my aunt, while Sophia listened intently to the description of John's father, a tall, courteous old man, with snow-white hair and piercing black eyes; of his kind-hearted Canadian wife, and the only daughter, for whose sake they kept open house, and gave the pleasantest balls and parties in all their circle.

"Susan Demeric has everyone asked there whom she likes, I know," exclaimed Sophia, with the pleased air of one whom some bright idea has just illumined. "Depend upon it she has taken a fancy to Captain Graham—that must be it!"

It looked like it, they all agreed, as they read on, while I hid my face behind the *Longfield Trumpeter*, and had to listen with loathing ears.

A glowing description followed of a visit the Demerics had paid to Ottawa, just as he happened to have been sent there on some special duty. It was only about a month before, towards the end of February, when it had taken place; and one day in particular was described, when, wishing to see the view, the party had ascended the tower of the government buildings, which stand upon the verge of the precipice, above the frozen river. The winter scene was depicted, when, as far as eye could reach, the sight wandered over one vast green field of pines, stretching away in solemn magnificence, save where the pure white of a snowy plain, beneath which slept the silent river, contrasted startlingly with its sombre verdure.

Then followed accounts of the Rink, of fancy balls, moonlight sleighing, and many another amusement, with frequent allusions to our cousin; unwitting signs, as we all declared, of an undercurrent of thought about her. We *all* declared—for I gave a sort of assent to what they said, while a sickening conviction that, just because the supposition was so intensely painful, it must needs be true, came over me.

"John says she certainly is very pretty, and was considered the reigning belle there last winter," said Sophia.

"And, you know, she is really quite an heiress, being the only other child, and they are so rich. Depend upon it, my dears, Captain Graham is *going in* for her," decided our aunt.

"I think you are all going rather too fast," said Nellie, in quite a cold tone.

"Nonsense, Nellie! Now what could be more evident? It is as clear as day." And Mrs. Burke read on with growing emphasis: "There is quite a marrying fever among our fellows out here; and in all likelihood a good many of us will be done for—certainly the Canadian ladies are wonderfully pleasant. From all accounts the same epidemic prevails over with you; so it is on the cards that, before this year is out, nearly all of our jolly circle at Ballymore last summer will be made happy for life. I hope so, for one, anyway, most heartily."

"There, that is pretty plain," quoth Mrs. Burke, in triumph. "If they are not already quietly engaged, you may be sure that they understand each other."

"Perhaps they are afraid of objections, and think when John goes over he will take their part, and I shall most certainly do my best to promote it," exclaimed Sophia. "How strange you two are!"—turning to us. "I declare neither of you takes the slightest interest . . . and yet last summer you both made much more of Captain Graham than I did. Well, *I* am not a summer friend, at least."

"Nor am I. But until one is certain of a thing, I see no use in supposing it," retorts Nellie, with slight sharpness—perhaps the result of our elder sister's pharisaical assumption.

Bitterly grateful am I in my heart to her for that curt reply, and give a long envious glance at her from behind my newspaper as she moves to the piano. How trim and neat and pretty her figure looks in that black walking-dress, whose colour contrasts so well with her fair hair and happy fresh face! Would she look as well and happy, I wonder, if Bob were to treat *her* as—*This will never do*—I must get away—anywhere! Just as I gain the door, trying to move carelessly, though feeling as if some one, hitherto loved and trusted, had just given me a sudden, stunning blow, Nellie's voice sings out gay and clear,

"Blue eyes or brown eyes, hazel or gray,
What are the eyes which I drink to to-day?"

Something between a sob and a stifled laugh answers as I close the door, and rush upstairs to my own room. And there what do I do? With a feeling of such utter wounded misery as I have never felt in all my life before—not were all the vexations, sorrows, and annoyances of my young years to be heaped together—I stand in dumb wretchedness on the hearth-rug—stand there, cold and silent, as if stiffened to stone while at once my future, my life, the whole world has grown cold and grey, and in my mind there is nothing but blackness, as of night, settling down. "How could he? Oh! how could he?" is all my pale lips mechanically frame; then, with a sudden impulse, I turn to the glass and look into it with a bitter smile. Nellie is fresh and blooming—she is happy in her love; while I—I—if that is the Queenie Demeric of last summer, what wonder he should care for some brighter face than that which, haggard, white, with close-set lips and miserable eyes, stared back, well-suited to that deep crape and mourning black dress.

"Blue eyes or brown eyes, hazel or gray?"

My grey eyes are dim and misty, and framed in red lids—the effects of many a night's silent tears for my dead boy; but those tears did not hurt as does this dry-eyed misery. It was not only the child's death either which has made me grow daily thinner and paler, but also that parting in October. Against one I could have struggled, but both griefs have almost beaten me down. "Oh! Harvey, Harvey, how could you write it? So soon, too—so soon! 'What are the eyes which you drink to to-day?' Not mine!—not mine!" And I covered my face with cramped, cold fingers.

What humiliation is greater than such slighted love? What misery equals that of finding one's trust thrown away—wasted? One's whole heart taken up gently for a moment, then thrown with smiling carelessness aside? "I could never have done it to you—never!" And a wondering surprise came over me that, since he had loved, he could possibly hurt me. Then I thought of that night when we parted, and how he said that for years he could never think of another. Had he not said we should meet again—*there?* Was this the goodness which had made me feel ashamed of earthlier feelings, and resolve to look higher, onward and upward? Then, as the worst phase of all followed—that of distrust and doubt of all and everything, since he in whom I had so utterly and entirely trusted had failed me, my pride broke, and, sinking down on the floor, I wished myself insensible—dead; that this unbearable misery should be crushed out, even if it left me senseless dust and ashes.

For some time I was all but mad from my love and misery and wounded pride.

"'But that the fear of something after death'——" I muttered to myself, while hot, big tears fell thick and fast on that square of carpet at which I stupidly tried to stare as it rose up and danced and swayed before my misty vision. "If one's after-life were a nought, a blank—if I could die a dog's death, with no soul or memory to haunt me through eternity—why, I *would* die—*now!*" Not Christian sentiment? Of course not; but I feel crazed. Was it not hard enough to bear before, when thinking of my long weary life?—but this is ten million times worse! Why—why, when at least I was trying to bear it cheerfully and resignedly, do such things come to make the whole world seem full of tears and misery? "We know not now, but we shall know hereafter —hereafter!" And rising, I drag myself slowly to the window, to look out and see —yet not see—the bare, wintry face of the earth, with a subdued, cold gleam over it, as of a coming ungenial spring.

A bitter east wind blew over the land, and looking away through the stiff elm-branches, cold, light-grey clouds swept softly and swiftly across the sky. Something slipped from under my elbow as I leaned upon the dressing-table. My Bible! and looking, I laughed—actually laughed—but it turned off into a bitter sob that tightened the muscles of the throat.

"Some people would tell me that is comfort even for such sorrow as this, but it is not—it is not. How could I desecrate a prayer with such a tale of earthly unhallowed grief as mine? I was trying to be resigned—good—from a wrong motive, and my sin has found me out. And now—now he would be *hers*, even beyond the grave! Holy griefs and sorrows are mentioned here, but where any love-sick misery like mine? Was human nature different then, or would such selfish woe have profaned those pages? Yes, yes, that must be——"

There is a step in the passage outside, and in one instant I have composed myself, and stand looking expectantly at the door; but it passes; then, remembering that the rest meant to drive over to one of our neighbours for luncheon, I resolve to slip quietly outside, away, so soon as they go, free from curious, prying eyes.

In about half an hour the carriage-wheels rattled in the court-yard, and then rolled round to the door; so, listening till the rumble died away, I hastily pulled on a jacket, and, seizing my hat, with a thick veil, to hide all traces of tears, stole outside to the Fir-wood, and there paced up and down, up and down, as I did so often when November's leaves lay thick on the path; and my thoughts, if sorrowful, were yet far easier to bear. Cold as was the day, there was still a breath of spring in the air. Here and there a few stray larches were showing sprays of soft green, tufted feathers and faintly-pinkening cones; some yellow primroses, sheltered by their strong, coarse leaves, glimmered temptingly among the dark rocks down by the pool, and the rocks themselves were covered with moss, whose dark winter verdure was relieved by tender green sprouts.

Looking at the pool, whose depths were dark as ever from the shadows of trees whose branches knew little winter or summer change, I think over all the associations of the place; of Davie's funeral, when that black line wound round by here to the churchyard which nestles on the other side of the wood; before that, those days in dark November; earlier again, my quarrel with Dudley Wyverne—Dudley! "Would he—he—have acted in this way? Was not his love sober earnest, and no mere passing fancy? Hush, hush! Could I be already so changed in my creed as this?"

A sort of rushing sound, as of a wind in the tree tops, made me look up suddenly, but not a branch of the sheltered larches swayed;

then, looking still, a dark torn stripe of cloud was wafted rapidly overhead with a quick, whirring swish: it was a great flight of plover, seaward-bound, and the sound was the beating of their countless little wings. Leaning my arms on one of the rocks, I watched it listlessly, as the cloud lengthened out, grew swallow-tailed, and wavered into curves in onward flight, then breaking into three flocks passed away to the sea, their dark bodies growing smaller and smaller, till they seemed mere separate specks in the distance.

The sight of those birds somehow did me good by arresting my attention and breaking that morbid, sick train of thought. Turning all of a sudden, I walked straight back towards the house. What? Should I, Queenie Demeric, who had always inveighed with such scorn against people nursing their love sorrows, and making their lives a misery to those around them—was I to break so weakly down? What would not Aunt Emily think, were she to return and find the orders never given, the notes unwritten, which were but part of my daily task? So with an effort—a great one—I had to come back, as bravely as might be, to the common prosaic round of life, though all seemed so changed for me. And I did it: I bore up stoutly till that afternoon near evening, when some chance words of Sophia's, as she turned from her writing, overcame the frail barriers all of a sudden.

"Do you know what news I am telling John? Why, that 'Sunbeam,' as they call Susan, has evidently kindled *a flame.* Captain Graham used to like talking to you rather, Queenie; so he is only transferring his admiration to another of the family."

Sophia never dreamt of hurting me by her careless raillery; never perceived that my cold air was assumed as I rose, saying only, "Did he talk much to me? Well, past is past, and one's admirers of last summer are as old-fashioned as one's dresses . . . The freshness of both is gone,"—but Nellie's quicker eyes had seen me wince.

Once more I sought refuge in my own room.

"I wish we had never met," I said fiercely, sitting down in a low wicker chair and burying my face in my hands; then more softly, "Oh that we had never met, or that I had died first, not knowing it! Had he died first, though, I could have kept true for ever."

"For the saddest of love is love grown cold,
And 'tis one of its surest phases;
And far better than Life, with two hearts estranged,
Is a low grave starred with daisies."

Why would that keep rhyming on and on in my weary brain, while every tone, every change of his face and voice, as he sang it long ago in the Autumn gloaming, came back to my mind. How long ago?—only one half year!

All in a moment I seemed again as then in the drawing-room, seeing between the curtains twilight glimpses of the garden outside; the fire rose and fell, sending out bright jets of flame, which lit for an instant the faces and the grouped figures, then let them relapse again into pleasant, warm darkness.

Away in the corner the white keys of the piano glimmered ghostily, and by-and-by I rise, yet linger still a while to join in the talk; then finally, gliding on to the music-stool, strike a lingering chord or two doubtfully in the semi-darkness. Then —ah! then—another voice joins with mine, or, it may be, sings alone those songs which I have hated to hear ever since. How it all comes back again ; a touch of the hand as we turned the leaves ; a look as the fire showed our eyes meeting for a moment—mere nothings, yet how happy, how miserable they made me, believing as I did that this was all I should have my whole life through to think of and look back upon ; and that since it must be so, I could be content, having at least the sure knowledge of his love.

"And now, is this man a lunatic, or for what did he take me? Does he think me deaf, or dumb, or blind—dead to all feelings of weak human nature—that he writes this happy letter full of his rides and drives and parties—sleighing by day, dancing by night with her, as he used with me? And writes it all with the mention of the Demerics and of her pervading every line, evidently expecting me calmly to accept the situation! Why, it's *amusing*, you know, if one could only take it in that light."

So I rave on and on in the same fatal circle of thought, which is too strong to break. A step comes to the door; a little, apologising knock. It is Nellie—good little Nellie, who in general never knocks; so, foreseeing that she guesses at my state of mind, I summon pride to my aid, begin vigorously washing my hands, and cry, "Come in!"

She entered quietly, with a look of consolation all over her small person, and walking softly, as if I were ill, fixed her eyes upon me with a gentle, sorrowful stare.

"What is the matter?" I testily ask, hardening my heart against her silent sympathy. "Are you moon-struck?—or what necessity is there to look at me as if I were something odd in natural history—a—a woolly rhinoceros, or a cave-bear?"

"Oh, Queenie dear, I am *so* sorry! He need not have written like that . . . it—it was not kind, I think, after the attentions he showed you——"

"Why, that is the joke of it, don't you see?" I cried, interrupting her with a short laugh, and the forced sound startled myself; it seemed such a strange thing to do. "It is nothing to me, my dear, you see, when I can laugh over it."

But my sister looked unconvinced, and something gathered in the corners of her grey eyes—Nell cries very easily.

"There, there," I beseechingly added. "For Heaven's sake, don't pity me, or I shall cry next! It will be all the same in a hundred years; only *don't* pity me, dear." Then, in some anxiety, "Aunt Emily does not guess anything is wrong, does she?"

"She has been calling at the top of her voice for you without moving from her desk," angrily answered Nellie, "just as if she expected you to live tethered to her chair. She says, dear, that of course the orders were all wrong while you have been housekeeping for her lately, and that no one but herself can do anything right. Shall you mind coming down, dear?"—soothingly. "Indeed I am afraid you had better."

"Oh, I'll go," with a great effort. "Let me see how my eyes look, though. Good heavens! I am a beauty!" was my next grim exclamation, on beholding in the glass a reflection with red eyes, tossed hair, and a white swollen face. "No, it's no use, Nell. I *can't* show myself for half-an-hour yet."

"'If the mountain doesn't come to Mahomet'—why, then, the other thing will happen, you know;" and with this apt quotation, my sister seized some rose-water, and proceeded to deluge my face and dress, gave three violent tugs at my skirts, as if they were in fault, and finally brushed my hair with such vigour that I put up my hands in self-defence, when, dropping her instrument of torture with a clatter, she decisively said,

"There, you'll do!"

I don't feel as if I would do; but go I must. Already as we opened the door a shrill cry of "Queenie!—Qu-ee-nie!" resounded up the stairs, denoting clearly that Mrs. Burke was under arms, and not to be trifled with. So, slowly descending, I encased myself in that mail of cold reserve and stiff-neckedness which we sisters all assumed as the only armour proof to resist our respected relative's onslaughts.

"Well, upon *my* word, Mary Demeric, I shall not stand this much longer," was her greeting, as I entered, and advanced to the davenport, behind which she was enthroned in regal wrath, brandishing defiantly a steel pen for sceptre, while bills were fluttering all over desk, chair, and carpet; for, to add to the discomfort which generally surrounded her presence, the window was open —since she delighted in fresh air—and the cold rush of wind chilled me to the bones. "It is always the same with you girls," she continued, breathing hard, with what seemed intended either for noble scorn or righteous indignation. "Pretending to help me, but only ordering here and ordering there, with the most careless extravagance, while my life is worn out going after you and countermanding every single thing. Will you have the great kindness to explain to me," she continued, mincingly, with an attempt at cutting composure, which almost upset me into an hysterical laugh by its absurdity—"Will you condescend to inform me what this means—and this—and this? All orders of yours, I suppose, of which I know absolutely nothing," and in a white heat of mixed anger and triumph she flourishes bill after bill before my eyes. "Oh! I declare," breaking down into the hot stage again, "you make me perfectly wild with your primness and cold ways, Mary."

Very quietly I turned the leaves of my household books, and with inward thankfulness pounced upon two lucky slips of paper, which convicted her in her own writing of having herself given me these orders. We sisters have made a quiet practice of doing nothing without such permission, since first we discovered Mrs. Burke's inconvenient absence of mind, which made her, in all good faith, quite forget many of her own words and actions. Slowly now her pen came down from its airy position; her lips framed an "O-oh!" The laurels of her premature victory were fast shedding their leaves, and quite mildly fell her disconnected syllables.

"Ah! . . . is—that—it? . . . I see-ee. Well, why could you not have said so sooner, instead of letting me fuss my poor brain into such a headache?"

She ended with a sigh of peevish reproachfulness; then, suddenly, with renewed strength, and almost joy, returned to the charge.

"And of course not! No, I am certain you never once thought of it, though I begged you. Oh, never! Of course you never scolded the butcher about sending such old tough beef, and your uncle will be annoyed again, and I shall have a headache—it is always——"

"I *did* tell him," I reply, in exasperation. "On Wednesday last, when I was riding, I stopped there and sent in for him."

"Well?" in expectation.

"'Mr. Murphy,' I said, as severely as possible, 'Mrs. Burke is excessively displeased that you sent her such tough meat last time, and if it should occur again she will certainly be obliged to leave you.'"

"And what did he say for himself?"

"Say! He grinned from ear to ear, and kept pulling at his dirty cap. 'Troth, miss, and it was a Methusaleh, sartinly, and so I tould his honour's man, when I tuk the baste off his hands.'"

"It was none of ours, surely?"

"Indeed it was," and I felt a bitter satisfaction at her dismay. "'Ah! now, blessin's on ye, Miss Demeric, dear,' said Dennis. 'Shure I never tuk into account the misthress would have the heart to object to her own mate!'"

Our little duel over, I remained downstairs, for so long as I can I would fly from the thoughts which come with solitude; but Mrs. Burke's attacks left a disagreeable impression behind of having been roughly shaken, vulgarised, and lowered. Such outbreaks recurred periodically, and seemed like safety-valves, so essential to her well-being that, when the thunderstorm had been longer than usual in brewing, we used privately to think it had a bad effect upon her health.

My feelings just now would have been far easier to bear could such grief have flowed quietly, without the terrible strain of keeping up appearances. But that could not be, though I longed for a whirl of excitement and wild gaiety; to laugh, talk, dance, flirt myself out of this agony of hurt, pride, and affection; or at the least to still its voice. How often must one descend instead from the heights of passion to the table-land of every-day life, and do exactly all one has been doing during almost every day of the past three hundred and sixty-five, as if no fierce storm had swept over that quiet plain of one's existence, uprooting and breaking down the landmarks which have grown part of one's inner life. The daily round is precisely what then requires most real courage to accept; if, but with outward cheerfulness, yet with inward resignation; still how many women there are who do accept and patiently endure it to the end, with smiling, yet tired faces and sore hearts? While, on the contrary, how many men whose seas of trouble are in reality no deeper, though rising perhaps to a higher fever-tide of passion, reject such endurance as tame, and think no shame to inflict the effects of their recklessness and passionate impulses on those around them.

Here and there among those names so thickly inscribed in the roll of our memory, can we not recall a sad few who, in some fit of momentary despair, have cursed their luck and tried to drown and deaden memory and thought in those waters of Lethe which flow on all sides with such fatal temptingness, and so going step by step down a twilight social descent, are shrouded in gathering gloom, till little by little they fade out of our daily speech and life, and almost memory. Then, it may be, some day we overhear two old college friends, or school-boy chums, talking together of pleasant by-gone days, who, disinterring old happy memories, covered with the dust of busy years, ask with awakened interest after the once familiar name which has lain silent for so long.

"What, did you never hear? Came to utter grief, poor fellow!" is the carelessly-pitying answer. "Debts, duns, difficulties—no end of troubles. Was jilted, too, and took it to heart. Friends made him ex change, and he went to the West Indies first, and then to the d—l."

"You don't say so?" replies the other, with a sigh, maybe. "Poor old Fred, or Bertie, or Cecil," (as the case may be). "What a ripping good fellow he was!"

Such a tale is rare, perhaps. But why should women still more rarely break down under added woes? Not that their feelings are shallower, not because they are more fenced in from temptation. Is it that to these feeble ones of the earth is graciously given that higher courage—the courage not to *do*, but to *endure?*

So, to return to myself after this digression, I remember indistinctly that I spent the evening as usual among the others, trying to deceive Nellie's loving vigilance by taking more than usual interest in trying new music, or some fresh stitch in my lace-work, while humming a bar or two. The air is not musical, as little Nora takes care to inform me from the fender-stool, where she is hugging her kitten, attired in Dolly's clothes, which it resents by feeble mews.

"What is that be-ootiful tune, Queenie? You are singing it so funny. Hush! pussy! One more miaow, and you shall have a cold bath and go to bed."

It was after dinner, and at this point (to my relief and that of the unfortunate kitten, who had just had a wide paper collar fastened round its neck, and was forced to sit up and play at Queen Elizabeth), comes Lieschen to carry off her tyrannous little charge to bed.

"Come now, Fräulein Nora, *mein Herzblättchen*," said that Teutonic damsel, with broad-faced suavity; but catching sight of the unhappy little nursery pet, her countenance changed, and snatching up pussy, she tragically exclaimed—"Ach, mein Fräulein, wie *ist* es möglich, und wie ist est *nicht* möglich!"

"Come and say good night when I am in bed, Queenie. Remember, now, Queenie!" called out the unwillingly-departing little lady as the door closed upon the trio.

Her request was well-timed, for my nerves

felt as if they might give way at any moment under that constant strain, so in a few minutes I rose to follow her.

The March twilight had lasted late, so, as yet, there was no lamp in the gallery nor in the hall below; night is coming on, however, and its darkness is closing down fast all over the land. Out in the hall the shadows were lying thick and deep; the only light came faintly through the large painted window on the stairs, where shone in gules and azure the arms of the Demerics. A distant clock in the servants' offices slowly struck the hour. What was there in the sound, the darkness, or the memory these brought, which made me shiver and draw a long breath? For one moment I leant my forehead against the sharp edge of the oak door, and stood as on *that* night, wrapped in the gathering darkness. So, once before, I had stood on the same spot, in similar friendly shadows, hearing the same sounds; but *then* an arm was round my waist: I was leaning on his breast—my God! I sprang away with a silent cry and a feeling of horror. How I loathed that spot! Never more would I touch it—*never.* At this very moment, perhaps, he was telling her the same tale, or they two might be standing face to face in happy, golden silence!

Catching hold of the heavy oak rail of the stairs, I looked up for a moment to the shimmering window with a wild invocation in my heart against the falseness, the cruelty of it all. The little light seemed concentrated in the coloured glories of those panes, shining softly between their heavy-mullioned framework; while higher up, in the arch of the window, glowed dimly the arms which our ancestors had bravely borne against the

Saracens, in toiling marches and bloody strifes, on the hot sands of Palestine; the crest a hand grasping a bloody cross, while there was still light to read beneath plainly their old motto—"Dieu m'aydant je porte la croix." *La croix!* They could bear their crosses bravely, while I—I——

The sight of that motto brought the tears suddenly to my wearied eyes; but also a sense of help and relief to my wearied heart. Instead of going first to the nursery I went once more to my own room, and there, throwing myself on my knees in the darkness by the bed-side, cried out all my aching and pain and sorrow. Womanly pride would not let me disburden my heart to even the most loving earthly ears, for any sympathy would have been yet more galling than the wound—so, by clasping closely, the grief would have hurt deeper and still deeper had I not so thrown it down, and, looking at it boldly, seen what and how much it was, and asked for help to endure it. It was but a light cross surely, yet instead of moaning and wincing dumbly, was it not better to join mine to those voices that go up night and day crying for help and strength in their daily troubles and trials and woes. Ay! even this, added to Davie's loss, was yet but a small cross compared with those of others.

"Dieu m'aydant *je la porterai.*" And when I rose up and went, quieted and comforted, into the nursery, Nora could hardly keep her sleepy eyes long enough open to kiss me.

CHAPTER III.

THE TIME OF THE SINGING OF BIRDS.

"Little brings the May breeze
Beside pure scent of flowers,
While all things wax and nothing wanes
In lengthening daylight hours.
Across the hyacinth beds
The wind lies warm and sweet,
Across the hawthorn tops,
Across the blades of wheat."

IT is two months later; and my two sisters are married. The young May moon, which Ireland's Anacreon used so rapturously to address, is beaming down on an Irish landscape once more, and probably shedding as silvery a haze, equally subtle, love-inspiring influences over the sea, terraces, croquet-ground, and masses of white hawthorn and heavy-flowering lilac bushes of Longfield, as ever she did over Morna's witching grove. Unfortunately for the poetry of the occasion, however, I am only sitting at the window of Mrs. Forbes' pink guest-chamber, enjoying the warm, mysterious beauty of the Spring night, with my hair falling loosely over a white dressing-gown; am also prosaically thinking how sleepy I feel, and wondering why Bella has not yet come for our bedroom chat, which, feeling lonely without my sisters, we have held since this my solitary visit commenced.

"Come in—I was just meditating on my lost beauty-sleep," I said, yawning widely, as the door opened, after a quick tap; then, hearing no answer, turned to see the cause of such unusual silence, and exclaimed, in utter astonishment, "*The Saints preserve us!*"

There stood Miss Forbes, with a grin of the most absurd self-satisfaction on her merry countenance, arrayed little below the knees in a gorgeous albeit naughty crimson petticoat, over which her dress was puffed up; a pink-edged bath towel elegantly crossed over her chest; two peacocks' feathers adorning her high felt hat, and a walking-stick grasped sturdily in her hand.

"Mother Hubbard, my dear. How do you like me?" she demanded, turning herself round and round for inspection, as I went into convulsions of laughter over the want of growth of her petticoats and her sturdiness of limb. "Isn't it killing? They are things of grandmamma's I poked out the other day; and see, here is a court train for you," and she dived at a black mass on the ground. "I want to startle the others out of their senses, so pull it over a white silk slip and come along."

The hour was about half-past eleven—a fitting time for such midnight pranks; so a few minutes later beheld me also tightened in an old-fashioned, peaked, high-body, and ruffled sleeves, and a black velvet train, turned back with white satin.

"Oh! Bella, Bella, what wasp-waists they must have had in olden days," I gasped, while straining my fingers at antipathetic hooks and eyes which steadily refused to meet.

"Yes, indeed, but their stays must have been of steel and buckram, I always think, or surely flesh and blood would have resisted." And Bella, with a smothered sigh, glanced at her own stoutly comfortable dimensions in the cheval-glass. "Come now, young woman, are you ready? You look quite lovely," she abruptly continued. [" I declare the vanity of the girl is astonishing. Does she mean to stay all night admiring herself?"]

This last was a sort of moral aside, delivered in reproof, as I turned myself this way and that before the mirror, studying the very becoming effect of my borrowed plumes.

"It would do for Mary Queen of Scots, only that my hair is down," was my answering remark; giving one final glance over my shoulder at the sweep of my retreating magnificence.

"Never mind your hair," quoth Bella, opening cautiously the door. "It looks quite *pictury*, so come along."

Out into the corridor we proceeded, and down the stairs, where every step creaked ominously as we went on tiptoe, in dread of poor Mrs. Forbes' bewilderment should she open her door and behold us?"

"You don't think we shall meet any one, do you?" I whispered, peering over my flat candlestick. "I wish heartily your sisters were not in such an out-of-the-way corner."

"Who is there to see us except papa or Gerald?—and they are either in the smoking-room, or they ought to be in bed."

"Hush! Listen!" and at the foot of the stairs we both stood, almost tragically, in sight of the haven of refuge—a door on the other side of the hall, leading to the young ladies' wing—but between us and which opened another door, leading to the sanctuary of the great goddess Nicotine. Steps and men's voices were sounding along that passage, and the next moment saw us scurrying up the stairs again, like frightened rabbits. "In here," I breathlessly whisper, pulling Bella behind the heavy curtains of the staircase window, and blowing our candles out just as the door-handle below rattled.

"How my heart beats! Don't you feel like a thief?" gasped Bella, panting, in my ear.

"Hu-ush! I should never forgive you if they beheld me such a spectacle!" I whispered sternly back, though smothering a laugh in my handkerchief, and trying to peep with timid care between the curtains.

"Why, bless my soul! it is later than I thought!" said old Mr. Forbes' voice, as he and his son came up the stairs; the elder man wearing an old shooting-coat over his usual evening nether garments; the younger in a grey-striped smoking costume of fantastic design and braiding.

Just as they approached us we heard them stop, and, dreading discovery, we caught each other's hands in the darkness.

"'Pon my honour, I can't find my pocket-book, Gerald."

"Shall I see if you left it beside the lamp, sir?"

"Ah, do, do, there's a good fellow," and a retreating noise is heard down to the smoking-room.

Choking our breathing in our handkerchiefs, and trying neither to move nor laugh, we both remained within a yard of the good old gentleman's unconscious nose, counting every moment till Gerald came back again, taking two steps at a time as he bounded up the stairs.

"Oh! I *do so* want to sneeze!" murmured an agonised voice close in my ear.

"Don't *dare to do so!*" was the ferocious,

though smothered reply. "Rub the bridge of your nose—rub hard."

"What is that noise, Gerald?"

I seized Bella's arm, and pinched it wickedly, to keep her quiet—so wickedly that she removed her handkerchief to remonstrate, and burst forth immediately with a loud "*A-tish-u!*"

"Who's that?" cried the father.

"Who's there?" demanded Gerald, springing forward.

"Oh! there's nothing left but to put a bold face upon the matter," thought I, so answered meekly, "Please, Mr. Forbes, it's the cat."

"Cat, indeed!—a pretty pair of cats!" as, dashing aside the curtains, they discovered us in our embarrassing situation, Bella shaking hysterically, with her long repressed laughter; while I vainly endeavoured to cover my confusion by a dignified curtsey to the dear old man, the effect of which, with my hair about my shoulders, added to my peppered and dusty velvet splendours and laughingly piteous face, sent both gentlemen—the one into his usual cackling cachinnation, the other into hearty peals of laughter. Nor were we allowed to escape till we had faithfully promised to display ourselves again on the morrow, for the edification of the entire family.

"What a pair of idiots they must have thought us, Arabella," said I, when we were once more safe in my bedroom.

"Oh! my dear, you are such a favourite of papa's, that everything you do is perfection; and as to me, I don't care. There is no fool like an old fool, and I am ageing very fast."

So saying, Miss Forbes shrugged her

shoulders, and gave a self-depreciatory stare in the glass.

"And your brother?" I asked doubtfully, shaking the sainted Mistress Forbes' finery in a mass round my ankles, my appearance suggesting a faint resemblance to a statue standing among ruins of bygone grandeur.

"Who cares what Gerald thinks?" answered my friènd, with an elder sister's mild contempt for a younger brother's opinions. "Do you know, though, Queenie, that he really took a great fancy to you last summer," she continues, meditatively trying the effect of Mother Hubbard's hat perched jauntily upon one hair, like the British officer's forage cap. "I don't mind telling you, as it did not last long, because others" (with a little laugh) "ran after you so much, he could never get a word in. Then he went over to Nellie, till Captain Kingston interfered *there*. What a pity there is not another of you, for he always says he admires the Demerics more than any other girls; and he is so difficult to please. Now I must go to my slumbers. Pleasant dreams, my dear, and a good night's rest to you," and therewith she departed.

The following morning rose bright and sunny with dewy freshness. It sees a bevy of young ladies walking up and down the drive in consultation; on either side the thick, freshly-springing grass of the lawn, studded here and there with milky hawthorn trees, being pleasant just to look at for its greenness this lovely May morning; for a soft wind is blowing; a warm sun shining; branches of tender pale-green beeches waving; and apple-blossoms, hawthorn, laburnum and lilacs scenting the air, and gladdening the eyes on every side.

> "When daisies pied, and violets blue,
> And lady-smocks all silver white,
> And cuckoo-buds of yellow hue,
> Do paint the meadows with delight."

A dark-blue sea in the distance; a fresh blue sky overhead—and below a green land all blossoming and bourgeoning; cattle on the hills; wood-pigeons cooing in the trees, and truant school-children birds'-nesting slily through the hedgerows! What more can be wanted to make such a day as this indeed one of those rare ones which caused the christening of the "merry month of May?"

We were consulting over some fanciful costumes in which we had agreed to astonish and delight Mr. Forbes and his quiet gentle spouse at dinner-time—such innocent amusements being dear to their kindly hearts; and, moreover, Bella and I had tyrannically declared that the other sisters must dress up absurdly to keep us scrapegraces in countenance.

The twin sisters, Effie and Emily, who came next in the family roll, required much persuasion to induce them to "make figures of themselves;" and observed, in slow *andante* tones, that "they did not see much fun in it."

At last, however, one was induced to personate a May Queen, with wreaths of pink and white hawthorn on her head, and white skirts—the other Spring, with a skirt looped over a green petticoat, and straw hat garnished with flowers. The remaining sisters gave us less trouble, since Bella considered the youngest her especial property, so, pouncing on the meek little prey, who never dreamt of opposing her despotic elder, she proceeded to array her as we both thought fit; and five o'clock that evening saw me busily powdering poor Maria's hair with flour procured from the kitchen, while Bella rouged her cheeks, and stuck on preternaturally huge black court-plaister patches. This done, we dressed her up in Bella's blue quilted petticoat and a beflowered print gown pinned up in bunches; told her she was at liberty to adorn herself further as she pleased, but on no account to dare to disarrange our handiwork; and—turning a deaf ear of cruelty to the poor victim's remonstrances that the plate-powder scarified her; the plaister drew the skin; the powder fell on her face, and that she was uncomfortable all over—we calmly assured her she looked charming, and proceeded to cool ourselves in my room, well pleased with our exertions.

"Oh, dear! What warm work that was!" cried Bella, seizing a fire-screen to fan herself and subsiding on the sofa.

"I am floury, hot, thirsty, and exhausted," was my self-pitying rejoinder; as I threw the window wide open and sank into an armchair beside it.

"I'll tell you what it is," said Bella, starting up with renewed energy. "We must have tea! We'll have it here and chat instead of going down to the drawing-room."

"Yes, *do*. Human Nature really requires support—at least that specimen of it with which I am the most intimately acquainted," I say, in tones of pleasant laziness. So Collins was dispatched on our errand, and we proceeded to hold confidential discourse over the generous allowance of refreshing bohea which was soon sent us from the housekeeper's room.

"Good, honest cups, I call them," said Bella. "Not the miserable little egg-shell things they give us in the drawing-room."

"I wonder if this will be a pleasant summer?" I say, after a time, lying back dreamily in my chair, with something of the lazy enjoyment of men, after having quieted their nerves by the soothing weed. "Though, indeed, I shall never enjoy any amusement in the future half so much now that Nellie and Sophia are married."

"Dear little Nellie!—what a pet she looked on her wedding-day! But you ought never to have allowed Sophia to cry her eyes scarlet in the way she did. I am so glad Gerald and I were asked to it, because it was my only chance, I suppose, of seeing them for ever so long," answered Bella, settling herself still more comfortably on the sofa, "though of course we should not have been vexed if you had not done so, knowing how quiet you all wished it to be. Do you remember how happy we all were last summer here? Do you ever see that pretty little vixen of a Mrs. Lascelles now?"

"Not so much, of course, since his death. Still she does not mourn inconsolably. He left her very well off, you know, and she lives at the Swiss villa as we drive into Maghrenagh."

A pause followed, which I broke by saying, rather dolorously,

"You can't think how changed everything seems to me since last summer. Sophia gone, and Nellie gone, and—and——"

"Yes, I know, dear," answered Bella, in soothing sympathy. "It must seem very strange. *We* don't change much, at all events.

"'For men may come, and men may go,
But we stay here for ever.'"

The application of this quotation meaning to denote that none of the five Miss Forbes have as yet been sought in marriage by any desirable wooer. I could hardly refrain from smiling at the probable truth of her last remark, but turned aside the inclination by a question.

"What first put it into your brother's head to go out to Canada this month, Bella?"

"Why, your own Canadian brother-in-law first did so, by hearing Gerald and Dudley Wyverne consulting about where they should take some trip together; and he urged them to go and spend the summer over there. Gerald has nothing to do, you know, and an elder son, without occupation, or even a hobby, is a pitiable object. Queer, is it not, that so many of our friends should go out there? Captain Graham there already, for one. How pleasant we all thought him, certainly!"

"Very pleasant," I answered, calmly. "But, after all, it is not surprising they should all be going there; one person often settles to go to some out-of-the-way place, and the novelty of the thing attracts friends."

What were my feelings since March with regard to Harvey Graham it would be hard to tell; perhaps it would be nearest the truth to say that I had endeavoured steadily never to think of him at all—had shut up a fallen idol in the deepest, darkest *oubliette* of my mind, resolving proudly never to unlock the door to gaze or mourn over the shattered relics—never even to ask myself whether, were the idol once more intact, I could worship it as of old. Perhaps not. It may be that wounded pride, in its strength, had suddenly dashed down what it would have required years for time or absence to undermine, and enabled me to think calmly and speak collectedly of the man whose mere name had once made my heart beat so quickly. I should always feel, always rejoice or grieve with him, never be able to quite think of him as like others; yet that I should ever again have just the same feeling, could we be once more together as of old, I knew in my heart was impossible, though not daring to think it boldly out. Yet his supposed engagement had never been absolutely confirmed.

"Yes, Captain Graham is there, and Sophia and her husband (they have arrived by this time)," continued Arabella, counting them off on her fingers. "And now Gerald is going, and Dudley Wyverne."

"Dudley Wyverne? You don't mean to say that—that Mr. Wyverne is going too?"

"Going! Why, of course he is. How startled you look!" answered my companion, with a quick glance, and a rather irritating smile. "Gerald and he settled it together, Too bad, is it not?—our nicest man; for half the rest are donkeys or detrimentals! But, goodness me, where on earth have you been, Queenie, not to know that before?"

"Living at Ballymore, where neither sight nor sound of outer world disturbs our blessed serenity. Going about among the people, and being happy in my own quiet way," I replied, with a little smile. Bella gave me a somewhat curious look.

"Do you know, Queenie, you are very much changed lately?" she gravely said.

"Am I? Well, let us hope it is for the better, then," with a slight laugh.

"Oh! yes, it is for the better." And Miss Forbes, rising slowly, prepared to leave the room. "I am only doubtful, my dear, whether it's not *too good to last!*" With which parting shot she made her exit.

"So even he is going away too. Now I shall feel more lonely than ever," was my first thought, as, left alone, I leant my head on my hand, and looked out somewhat desolately over the sunny flower-beds and terraces below, and away to the sea. Another screen seemed to have slid itself between me and the sunlight, not so black as those which had preceded it, but still dark, because I had just been basking in a faint, fitful gleam; because, also, it was so recently that I had been able to smile without effort again, to accept my lot cheerfully, without longing for more, because, simply, it *was* my lot.

It is trite, but none the less always freshly true, to say that one never knows the depth of one's own feelings for some beloved object till it is lost to us; but women in especial are apt to tyrannise over a silent homage rendered to them without fail; to receive carelessly, as a matter of course, that truest affection which never yet gave them cause for fear or jealousy. Let the incense, however, but seem to be blown by wavering breezes towards other shrines—let the hawk but break away for once, and fly down the wind as if exulting in his freedom—and the falcon will be caressed far more lovingly if it returns to its perch on the slender wrist, the incense inhaled twice as gladly when it is once more offered up. And though such general remarks as these could not apply to my case at this moment, still I had almost insensibly been so counting on seeing Dudley again, and had never seemed to imagine his possible absence, that now I felt personally aggrieved. Gerald Forbes I knew was to sail soon; my guardians had decided on spending the next winter abroad, probably therefore, I should not meet him again till the following spring, and even then he might have left Ireland. Perhaps it was better so—better for both of us; and I said to myself that I hated those dispositions which could not stand alone; which even if beaten down and repulsed must always turn with love to some other object on earth, trusting as blindly, believing as fondly as before, though perhaps not with the old warmth of fancy and imagination—I despised such foolish fondness which must cling its tendrils round *some* support, and again believe such immoveable. Could I not at least stand alone in my future life? How lately was it not that my mind had been saturated by grieving melancholy; occupied by the image of another man; and yet . . . . and yet . . . . . . Why would a small voice whisper insinuatingly close in my ear that first love might be sometimes ideal; that a second might be more real; that in the past days I had again almost unconsciously been dreaming dreams, building air-castles, with which had been associated shy thoughts, grateful memories, of the one person on earth who had never yet failed me.

"Not of course that I *love* Dudley Wyverne," I answered as lowly to that tiniest of whispers, "but I trust and believe in him so fully. And who can help seeing how different, how immensely above all the rest he is?"

Then, in self-excuse, I reflected that my girl's-love for Harvey had come naturally enough, since he was the first who had offered me admiration, liking and still warmer feelings which appeared all the more new and flattering compared with the accustomed everyday fondness of my sisters and the grumbling care-taking of our guardians, whose display of interest in us often took very disagreeable forms. It was as if some little Puritan maiden, scrubbing away amongst pots and pans, and toiling and bustling up and down over household duties, were to peep out of a window and suddenly there see a green, shady, mysterious garden she had never seen before, and become aware of a warmer scent-laden air playing round her hot, tired temples. She would draw in her head to scour and rub again with a sigh, thinking all day of that enchanted spot, and though in later years she might find herself free to wander at will through still more beautiful gardens, shadier alleys; and know that these were better and lovelier in every way, yet would still think sometimes with fond regret of that first peep into enchanted ground, which had seemed so strangely fair a view just because it *was* the first.

In those earliest days I had not even thought of loving Harvey Graham, knowing as I did, with my eyes wide open to the facts of the case, that that could only lead to unhappiness; but had imagined in my inexperience and love of castle-building, that a romantic friendship was not impossible; had even held before my own eyes all the while an outline of a later, different and more realistic attachment—in plain words to love and marry some other and be happy in the dim future; yet cherishing an affectionate regard for my first friend. Then, when we were both bound in the meshes, I calmly abjured this apparently ignoble thought, devoting myself in imagination to living for a memory; but those seemingly strong chains which were to keep us linked together despite intervening seas or ever diverging paths in life, were forged but by a girl's fancy, and secured to pillars of mutual trust and life-long attachment—let these only be roughly removed, and the whole, frail, connecting line would sink down suddenly, as if beneath the waves of that same separating Atlantic.

Had I always been able to think of him as constant, it is probable that for perhaps a long period I should have believed my love to be of that kind which is said to come only once and then for life-time; but that was past—my eyes were opened! and I knew now that, though still caring for Harvey dearly, I should have hesitated even were he still true, and that it were in my power to marry him—knew too, now, that I was fastidious, and that not many men, such for instance, as those who had suited my sisters so admirably, would have satisfied me.

Harvey's plain common-sense, the impress of his anxious conscientiousness, and his dogged way of sticking laughingly to his opinions, had first attracted my wayward, over-imaginative fancy; but that could not have lasted for ever. Without ambition, as he was, I must at last have felt in him the want of those qualities which could rouse my drowsy powers by the spur of affection into stirring usefulness and full activity. Fatally gifted as I was by nature with a keen insight into failings and weakness of intellect, it would have been impossible, despite much real and true affection, to blind myself to the fact that my talents and capabilities were superior to his. What I required was a master-mind to mine, with powers and shrewd good sense surpassing my own;

above all, with ambition and strong energies directed towards high and unselfish ends.

Of all my acquaintance Dudley Wyverne was the one man who had all this—the only one with whom I could not anticipate a faint weariness of common-places, an intellectual dissatisfaction creeping over my future life; but was I not deterred in honesty by the past, by that ill-fated, but only now most unhappy love which seemed to have blighted my life, from all thoughts on this subject?

Here Collins's entrance disturbed my self-colloquy, for Bella and I had agreed to dress early, so as to be cool before dinner. My costume had been shaken, and brushed, and furbished up by my maid, till she declared it to be "something more like the thing;" and when she had succeeded in arranging my hair over high puffs, with curls falling low behind, it was not so unlike the fancied Queen of Scots we had agreed I should represent.

"There!" said Collins, triumphantly, at last, seizing my skirts to give one final shake out, "you look quite splendid, Miss Queenie, I do declare." And she reached up to fasten in more securely, on one side of my head, a diamond star lent by Mrs. Forbes. "I always do say," she continued, letting her hands drop once more, and gazing me admiringly all over—"I always do say you look yourself in a real *clever* dress, and not one of them nasty skimping things."

So, fortified by this assurance, I proceeded downstairs, where the fourth Miss Forbes was calmly seated in the drawing-room, looking the primmest of Puritans in a brown stuff gown, and cap, apron, and cross-over, of white muslin. Having complimented her on the idea which she had carried out without divulging it to anyone, I turned to laugh and be laughed at by Bella, who just then entered with Gerald, and we all anticipated the astonishment of the curate, and the two old bachelor twins, younger brothers of Mr. Forbes, who lived close by, and were coming to dine.

"Come beside me, Mother Hubbard," I cried, gaily, determined that she must not guess my spirits had at all suffered by the news she had given. "We were partners in disgrace last night, so we ought to support each other to-day."

"Take care, Bella, she spoils your style of beauty," laughed her brother.

"I don't quite know that; but at worst I can be her foil." And Miss Forbes stoutly planted herself beside me.

"'When we came in by Glasgow town,
We were a comely sight to see;
My love was clad in the black velvet,
And I mysel in cramasie.'"

I appropriately quoted.

"Bella's costume is certainly original, and suits her down to the ankles. I don't say it suits down to the ground, because its length is decidedly curtailed," observed Gerald once more, with brotherly candour. "But your get up, Miss Demeric, is really becoming. Ladies always look well in black velvet. It will certainly fetch Wyverne when he sees it."

"Oh! I met him on the stairs, just as he came, and told him of our idea," said Bella, rather hurriedly.

"Met him! Met whom?" I ask, opening my eyes.

"Why, Dudley Wyverne. Did you not know? I brought him back from Z—— with me this evening." So saying, the crafty Gerald hunted at a side-table for a flower to adorn his coat.

I turned to look at the treacherous sister, but she was apparently admiring her shoe-buckles.

"You might have told me, Bella," I said, in a rather reproachful aside, to her.

"Told you? Told what?" and Miss Forbes looked up with the most beautifully assumed innocence.

"Oh! nothing," I answered, trying to disguise my awkward feelings by a little upward poke of the chin. "Only it seems so odd you should never have mentioned Mr. Wyverne when we settled to dress so ridiculously."

"Is it always necessary to tell one's guests who is coming?" demanded the young lady, in an injured voice; then added, more blandly, "besides, it would be impossible to know always whom Gerald may meet or bring home with him. I never thought either that you would mind what Mr. Wyverne thought of your appearance; but as you *do*, rest assured, for you look charming."

Much as things seemed like a little plot between brother and sister, they would clearly confess nothing. My mind was in a sudden whirl; I felt so angry with both, that I could have shaken them with pleasure; yet secretly a little glad, nevertheless; angry with myself for being glad, and with it all more nervous than I could have believed possible. No time was left to think, however, for in came Mr. Forbes, whose delight and astonishment at our travesties was so overwhelming, that we had to stand up and sit down, and be looked at all over, while he walked round and round us, rubbing his hands with satisfaction; the same performances, with slight variations, being subsequently indulged in by his little, old, rosy-cheeked bachelor brothers; and it was in the midst of a Babel of tongues that I caught the first sound of Dudley Wyverne's voice, which made me start, and talk most eagerly to my host, wishing very much all the while to turn round, yet not daring to look up till I heard him addressing me, when of course I shook hands, with quite a surprised air.

"What a charming tableau this is, that you have all got up for us," he began, in a mere complimentary, civil tone of voice.

"It was a surprise to hear that you were to be a spectator, at all events," assuming careless coldness.

"Why so?"

"Well, because I did not know you were here till a few minutes since."

"I beg your pardon, but dinner is ready

—dinner, dinner! Will you come, Miss Queenie?—Miss Demeric, I should say." And, offering his arm, Mr. Forbes cut short this friendly interchange of salutations, and carried me off to the dining-room, talking in short, chirrupy sentences all the way.

We had eaten and drunken, had toyed with dessert, and had then exchanged the dining-room for cooler air. Bella and I are walking up and down outside the windows, muffled in Galway cloaks, and talking busily, for it is my last night here, and we are now fast friends. We brush against branches of lilacs as we saunter to and fro; scarlet rhododendrons show duskily splendid behind the ribbon-borders, and white lilacs gleam coldly from shadowy corners of the shrubbery. By-and-by we hear steps crunching the gravel—men's voices apprise us of the comers before they turn the corner. The barbarous practice of sitting round a dinner-table till both men, in the dining-room, and ladies in the drawing-room, are sleepy and bored, did not prevail at Longfield. It was Liberty Hall, and Gerald and his friends might leave when they pleased; while Mr. Forbes soon followed, unless some of his country neighbours of the old school seemed inclined for a lengthened sit. Here they come in view. Gerald Forbes's tall figure, frightfully stooping; while his black eyes looked out from under their heavy brows with a gleam of malicious amusement. On the other side of the walk, Dudley lounged along, looking even handsomer than usual, every now and then throwing back his head with a low laugh; while between the two the stout, red-haired, little parish curate rolled towards us, looking from one to the other with an expression of pious horror, the skirts of his long black coat, many sizes too large for him, almost flapping against his heels.

"They are shocking the unfortunate little man almost out of his senses, as usual, I suppose," calmly remarked Bella. "Gerald's chief amusement is to uphold gravely some wild idea, which our poor little pastor never can answer at the time, though he is certain to denounce it with righteous horror from the pulpit next Sunday."

"Why should there *not* be sons of Ish as well as sons of Adam? Just hear the proofs, my dear fellow. Never reject any theory till you learn what can be said in its favour." And, from his tone and amused expression as he spoke, Dudley Wyverne had been clearly inflicting Adam and the Adamite on most unwilling ears.

"No proofs could convince me of the

truth of such a dangerous doctrine, sir-r!" responded the unhappy small divine, pursing his usually merry, fat countenance into a tight expression of horrified restraint—as who could fulminate thunders of orthodoxy to grind in powder these fantastical idea-mongers—yet mercifully refrained. "I sincerely trust your good sense will keep you from giving credence to these . . . ah—ahem . . . wild doctrines, Miss For-rbes," he admonishingly continued. "Mr. Wyverne here has been—hem!—promulgating the doctrine that we descendants of Adam are meant to educate the blacks, who were living —ahem!—previous to *our* cr-reation!"

"In that case, being all pedagogues, we ought to reverence our own Gamaliels in all cases," I remarked, demurely; and somehow Dudley interchanged a little side-glance of entertainment with me, which, like a secret understanding, drew us together, for the walk was narrow; while in front Gerald kept hammering away, hardening his new-forged beliefs, the protests of his awe-stricken little pastor growing fainter and fainter, the last we clearly hear being, "Why, now, sure, Mr. Gerald—sure, sir. Pause a moment! . . . Sir-r, my cawnscience—my cawnscience forbids me . . . ."

As if both unable to find a common subject, we paced in awkward silence along the broad terrace-walk overlooking the sea. At last Dudley forced himself to break the embarrassed spell upon us both.

"It seems a long time, does it not, since last I saw you?"

"It seems very long, certainly, though it is really not so many months since then," I answered, slowly, remembering with a tremor when that last painful meeting had been.

He bent his head slightly down towards me.

"You said you were surprised to-night when you saw me, but you did not say you were glad; you might at least say so now."

A pause, during which my wayward mind suddenly imagined his previous allusion was meant but to soften and touch my feelings, and render me more disposed to return his; so, in contradiction, I hardened my heart at once against his pleading, handsome face, answering coldly, despite a weak wish to tell the truth, and say I *am* glad,

"Might I? Well, yes, I suppose I might. Words signify so little one way or the other, don't they?"

"I think it is generally considered more honest to say what one means," he replied, shortly, straightening himself again.

"But society unfortunately will not allow of that," I continued, with mocking meditativeness. "Politeness and honesty can so seldom go hand in hand, and one must keep up one's pretty social fictions."

"Pray do not stain your conscience with more polite fibs, to me, at least, than you can possibly help," he replied, with growing shortness—fast becoming rather savage, though disdaining to show it, for my careless coolness irritated him keenly, while he little guessed what real nervousness it concealed; so he resumed, while raising his head and looking straight before him, "I should be very sorry to ask you to say anything you can't feel."

"Sometimes I don't seem to know what I feel or what I want; one's brain gets puzzled till it scarcely seems able to tell which thing it is one really *does* like or care for.

I don't suppose you can understand that in the slightest degree," I answered, breaking down suddenly from my former tone into an unconscious one of half-yearning: with an inward longing that I did know—now—that one way alone instead of two were open to me: that I myself could tell whether constancy to inconstancy, or a heart-weary refuge with tried affection, was what my inner self craved and dumbly asked for.

"No, I can hardly understand it: at least not from my own experience," he replied; but this time more kindly.

Once more we pace silently over the grey sea gravel; it crunches loudly under his heavy determined footsteps, more softly under mine, with an accompanying swish as my black velvet skirts trail heavily behind.

"I suppose you have heard of our trip to Canada?" he asked at length.

I nodded assent. "Yes. By the time you return we shall have taken wing also—we shall be abroad all Winter; probably not home till next spring again."

"*Really!*" and from his tone my news seemed to have disturbed rudely some plan or vision of his own. "I had no idea you were going . . . but, I hope you may enjoy yourself."

"Thanks. Canada is said to be so delightful, that of course you will do the same . . . the ladies especially are supposed to be most fascinating."

"So Mrs. Burke said, too, when I met her in town yesterday," he quietly replied.

If he wished for revenge he had it then, for I could not help wincing; my face changing; my heart growing sick within me, beating more rapidly for some quick, wild beats, then seeming to stop almost completely; knowing so well as I did all Mrs. Burke's garrulous tongue had told to the one man whose knowledge of it would so bitterly gall and humble me. I had been so tired of it all lately—of the wondering discussions held by Aunt Emily over all the last Canadian letters—of my own sore, wounded feelings, of my loneliness without my sisters—that I suddenly became conscious of a great humiliating wish to accept that affection which I felt Dudley was offering me, to burst out crying, tell him all my troubles,—be at rest and have done with it all. And I would have done so then,—would have broken weakly into the repressed sobs which heaved my chest, evoking surely all the pity and the love which he had been struggling to keep back, and so this history would have had an ending here,—but that my woman's pride came to my aid. He must not think me ready to turn to him only because Harvey Graham had transferred his affection elsewhere—a shuttlecock thrown back by one player and flying towards the other. Even if he had sufficient love to take me in such a fashion, what would he think of me in his heart? Would he ever understand, what was yet true, that alongside of my love for Harvey there had been subtly, quietly, growing up feelings for *him* which I could hardly analyse; fullest confidence; blindest trust; and *more*—which—which made me long that I dared accept his love as the highest earthly good I could dream of; yet I must not do it. Even if he were chivalrous, quixotic enough to forget all that he knew of my feelings and doubts and uncertainties, how could I allow him to take up so worthless, so rejected a gift?

If only I could know what was in his

mind when he sent that slight, yet most piercing shaft about Canada; whether smiling pity for my misplaced infatuation; or honest sympathy; or simply a wish to see how I would take it—but people may often long to read each other's souls, and yet, looking eyes into eyes, can never guess half the subtle thoughts which we hardly dare own to ourselves—far less to even our nearest and dearest; so perhaps he was imagining at equal hap-hazard the feelings which possessed me.

All these thoughts had passed through my brain, sweeping and rushing after each other with such bewildering rapidity, that in my confusion I fancied some trace of them must needs have shown in my face; and also that a dreadfully long silence had followed since Dudley's last words. And yet we had only walked gravely some yards side by side, to where, at the end of the walk, we had stopped instinctively to look at the view—one of the show spots at Longfield. An abrupt descent of rough hill-side beneath us, sloped into flat meadows, among which a shallow inlet of the sea wound lake-wise in and out, at the foot of the low, rounded hills opposite. Then it crept up to where a quicker river, babbling and hurrying down to meet it, burst its way between thick woods, which filled its native gorge, where lay hidden the house of the old Forbes twin brothers.

Suddenly Dudley spoke again, just as if no embarrassing silence had intervened, and we were both in so strange a state of mind that probably neither thought it odd.

"I never myself believed all the wonderful stories about the attentions Canadian ladies attract out there," he observed, without any *apropos*, raising his eyes to study attentively the rounded outlines of hills, rising like a pile of eggs one above another.

"Don't you?" was all I muttered, bending to gather up very carefully the long folds of my dress.

"No, I don't." Here he raised his voice decidedly, as if to convince himself also by mere force of sound. "And I should advise you not to credit them either. We all know—so must you also, though you have seen little of the world—how reports fly, and stories are invented and magnified. What might not people circulate, with a little exaggeration, about even you or I; so we ought to be slow in believing all we hear as gospel truth."

"Even if they are true, they are nothing to me."

"*Nothing!*" He turned quickly. "Are you sure of that—certain? Queenie! If he were standing there—*there*—on that side of the walk, and I, or—or anyone else here, would you not turn to him? Speak! Ah! tell me, just this once for all!"

And I—could only drop my hands despairingly on the little parapet wall, and look in hopeless uncertainty over the misty meadows.

"I don't know—oh! I don't know! I do so wish I did know! Have patience with me! Oh! don't be angry, for you are the only one of all left now, that—that cares!" . . .

I could not look at him.

"I see," he said, in a husky voice. "Don't mind my knowing it. You do care for him still, then?"

"No, no. At least, yes, but not in the old way. How can I explain? You see he was the very first who seemed to care much for me, and I was partly so pleased at that, while no one else was so very glad to be liked, even a little, by me. But now! —you know what they are saying, and I do, must, believe, from the tone of the letters, that—that"—here I paused, with my face painfully flushing; then, with a forced, joyless little laugh—"that his memory seems to have grown wonderfully short."

"What was it all? Can you tell me?"

"Ah! it was the whole spirit and tone." I smiled in contempt, not of him, but of my own vanity and romantic folly which had made me imagine myself worthy of being remembered; then humbly add, "They all wrote, too, it was not he alone—the Demerics also hinted plainly at his attentions to my cousin. Natural enough . . . I am not worth being cared for by anyone so long."

"It may be true; but all the same,

strange stories will get about without a particle of foundation," he answered, with some difficulty. "All might yet go well."

"Never! And even if it is not true, to what good could it all come?" I exclaimed, in despair. "It would only be fresh unhappiness. Oh! it was all a dreadful mistake; and I wish, oh! I do so wish I had *met you first,*" speaking out with a sudden wild impulse.

Dudley's arms were leant, like mine, on the low stone wall; he kept silent, with his head bent down, but his fingers were breaking off pieces of mortar, bits of lichen, crushing and flinging them down among the brambles on the other side, almost without knowing what he was doing. Rapidly I speak on.

"Don't you hate—despise me for being like this?—for being so fickle, inconstant? You would not believe me before when I told you that I was so. It was not true then, but it is true now."

"The cases are different," he slowly answered. "And besides," dropping his voice, "you do care still—in a certain degree."

"Yes, yes, but not in quite the same way, though I always shall care very much. See here, Mr. Wyverne," addressing him so suddenly that he turned his head with a start, looking into my dilated eyes, with our faces close to each other in the gray twilight, as I hurried out my words in an impetuous whisper, for otherwise heart and courage would have failed me to say them—"see here. You asked me whether I would go to him if he were there—beside us on the gravel; and I tell you I must go, and yet I should not wish to go. Even if it were all possible in the way of means and money, I should only go for the sake of what *has been*; feeling, knowing in my heart that it would not now content me; that it could only bring unhappiness. And I do so loathe myself for changing so quickly," I drearily continued, looking far away again. "So few months ago!—and yet during these last weeks I feel so altered. Yet he advised me, even begged me, not to remember—to forget."

Dudley gave a sort of groan of sympathy, self-pity, and disgusted misery.

"A saint might stand this, but flesh and blood can't!" he exclaimed, in self-exoneration. "*Queenie!*" and he made a sudden movement with his arm—but I had turned, too, looking, with a terrified face, down the long walk, up which our three friends were once more advancing; and Dudley, seeing them also, as quickly collected himself, facing the approaching figures with a scowl of detestation. Nervously hysterical as I was, his disappointed look touched some ludicrous chord, and I burst out in a faint laugh in his face. "What *are* you laughing at, Miss Demeric? I declare," putting down his heel into the ground with an angry, vicious dig, "I thought at least I understood *you* perfectly, but I can *not*. Of all the puzzling women——"

"I am sure it is no wonder if you don't." so I interrupt him, and this time with a great sigh, "for there is only one thing about myself of which I am absolutely certain, and that is, that I don't understand myself—no, not in the least. Ah! *don't* be vexed."

Dudley cleared his voice, which seemed somewhat hoarse, and then said hastily, but with decision.

"Don't you think our conversation

has been rather painful, and that we had better come to a clear understanding as quickly as possible. I have more patience than you perhaps think, and honestly I had intended to bide my time till after this trip—till the autumn—when time might have made things easier for you; but hearing you were going abroad then changes matters, and—Well, dear, I have gained more than perhaps I ought to expect, and after your return things must and shall be settled."

"I can promise nothing, remember."

"Never mind. Perhaps I know you better than you do yourself. You *do* like me?"

"*Yes,*" low, and with reluctance. "But, but listen, Mr. Wyverne!" as he turned away with an exulting expression.

"No. I shall not listen to another word—you have said it. Yes, Miss Forbes, it is a lovely evening, and certainly that view is charming down the valley there—beautiful."

"And the man had his back to it!" quoth Bella, raising eyes, voice, and shoulders in accusing witness; then reproachfully shook her head.

"How could I help doing so, when I saw Miss Forbes—even in the furthest distance," coolly replied her intended victim, with mendacious gallantry; whereupon Bella, uncertain apparently of how matters are standing, gave a disbelieving twist of her nose and sternly marshalled us all indoors.

The Longfield drawing-room wore still the same dark, blood-red appearance as of old, for though the wilderness of crimson satin furniture was protected by everyday cretonne coverings, these were of a still more sanguine hue. One lamp tried its best to light up the lofty apartment near the grand piano, on which two of the young ladies were playing a duet of tinkling little runs, the treble having the start of half a bar, while the bass tried vainly to catch her up; which performance, save for the name on the music cover, no one would ever possibly guess to be 'Figaro's Hochzeit.'

"There they are, play, playing away," observed Gerald to me with a confidential sigh, "and I do most solemnly declare I have heard nothing but that or Tancred for the last six months, morning, noon and night. Whenever I ask for something else I am told 'they must know something to play before guests.' But all the good of their practising, is to practise themselves in their faults."

Before the fire Mrs. Forbes, with closing eyelids and a sweetly placid smile on her broad but still handsome countenance, reclined peacefully in a low, deep chair, wherein she had comfortably disposed her ample person and matronly silk skirts, nodding all the while under the happy delusion that we believed her to be enjoying the music; while leaning on the mantelpiece and gesticulating (though carefully), with outstretched coffee-cups at each other, her husband and one of his twin brethren discussed animatedly the wholesome agricultural themes of top-dressing, subsoiling, and draining, with occasional digressing disputes upon the relative value of certain bone manures. Two more daughters, seated at another of the many tables, kept up a little quarrelling laughter over bézique with their most rosy-faced and favourite old uncle, who persisted in re-marrying his kings, overmarking his declarations, and chirruping while he rubbed his hands over all these delightful small trickeries.

"Do look at that very laziest of men!" exclaimed Bella, as her brother stretched himself on a sofa, with an air of extreme fatigue. "How on earth you will ever get him out of his berth, Mr. Wyverne, is more than I know, and as to leaving the settlements—you need never attempt it! Gerald would not be himself without kid gloves and a tall hat. It is the greatest pity he was not born a younger son."

"He shall go into the backwoods if I can manage it," quietly remarked Dudley to me. "I do get occasionally so heartily tired of society, and over-civilization. A little wholesome savagery does one all the good in the world sometimes."

"But I fancied you were so fond of society—you certainly go everywhere."

"So I do like society, and when I go in for it, go in thoroughly; but some natures require a thorough change at times, and I am a migratory animal, from habit and liking. I get so disgusted sometimes," he went on, confidentially, "so heartily sick with the miserably small jealousies of little cliques, and with the constant climbing up and kicking down on the world's ladder! One becomes misanthropic with studying too narrowly all the petty microcosms of society, which, after all, are only particles of the great whole; and then nothing sets me so much to rights again as regularly roughing it somewhere or other."

"But you don't really think badly of human nature, on the whole?" I rather blankly inquired, feeling that if my secretly-elected Gamaliel took this view, I too must follow it, though an unwilling disciple.

"I hope you don't think me such an utter prig as all that," he answered, laughing.

"Of course not; only at times one may get morbid, and take to looking at things through the wrong end of the telescope—of late especially."

The last was added in a low voice, and sent a quick thrill of pleasure through me, a momentary exultation in the power of swaying a stronger mind, even but in the slightest degree—a feeling which many a woman must have felt, even though never avowed; vulgar, if only delighted in for the sake of the evanescent feeling of power, but ennobling if looked upon as a means of producing effects for good, of which she is perhaps herself incapable. So, concealing a smile behind my fan, I think to myself, with some inward gratification, that perhaps he may not be morbid again for some time to come; that perhaps also I ought to be sorry, but I can't be; and that I am glad indeed that no one but myself knows how fickle my self can be—as of course I am.

"It only shows me more and more what a much easier life men have, and how much more patience we women need," I said aloud. "I might feel ever so much out of gear with social machinery in general, and yet I can't rush away for six months tiger-shooting in India, or for a trip to the South Sea Islands, like a man! A woman can only fold her hands, and try to practise the most difficult of all human virtues."

"Don't fret because you have a smooth, land-locked harbour to ride in safely, while we are tossing up and down on a rough sea outside."

"That is not a just comparison," I retorted, with spirit, an impatience of inaction stirring within me; looking straight forward with eager eyes at a reflected handsome man's figure in an opposite glass (which figure, by the way, is lying back and watching intently in its turn a close neighbouring reflection, the folds of whose black velvet draperies he almost touches, whose very fan quivers, the diamond star in whose fair hair seems tremulously gleaming, as if in unison with her impulsive nature, just now so highly-strung). "That is not just. It does not convey the right impression. Rather say that yours are ships in commission, free to sail from port to port—having liberty, freedom, action. We are only craft hauled high and dry on shore, rusting, moss-covered and lichened, in vile repose."

"A man achieves his greatest actions by doing; a woman hers by enduring. I thought that was your creed, and that you gloried in it."

"So I do—generally," I retorted, coming back, with a little puzzled shake of the head, to my old allegiance; "but sometimes it makes me a little wild to see men able to shape their own lives and move all about the world as I do so long to do; while I, because I can hardly migrate, as you call it, all by myself, must perforce sit still in my little corner, pick up any small straws of knowledge that may float by me on the current of life, but never embark on the stream and be carried down with it past unknown banks and fresh meadows!"

"That means that you are tired of living at Ballymore continually, and want change and travel, as you have so often told me," he quietly answered, as I paused, looking at me with the look and smile which always pleased and yet irritated me, because it read me so thoroughly.

"Yes; but that is not enough," I was answering petulantly, when down swooped Arabella upon us, as usual ruthless in the time and manner of her attacks, and tyrannically commanded Dudley to sing.

He hastily assented—perhaps as the quickest means of getting rid of her persistent importunities—then, turning to me once more as he rose, whispered quickly, with an exasperatingly glad expression,

"Who knows what may not be possible in some future day, my Queen?"

"What's that you were saying about my Queen—eh, Mr. Wyverne?" (What evil star could have brought that most terribly sharp-eared young woman behind us just then?)

"Oh, only asking Miss Demeric which arrangement of that song she liked best," answered poor Dudley, with an inward groan at the amount of fibs wherewith his conscience had been loaded in trying to elude her lynx-eyed vigilance.

And, whether it was in righteous retribution for the sin, I know not; but the uncompromising Arabella sternly presented him with that self-same piece of music, which he was naturally obliged to sing through to the end for her benefit.

"And I give my heart to my lady's keeping,
And ever its strength on mine I shall lean;
And the stars shall fall and the saints be weeping,
Ere I cease to love thee, my Queen, my Queen!"

Those were the words which kept ringing through my ears that night, as with bewilderingly opposed feelings of self-reproach, joy, shame, gladness, I laid my head on the pillow—words which were destined to sound in them again for the next night, and the next, and many a long night after.

CHAPTER IV.

IT NEVER RAINS BUT IT POURS.

"And the palpitating engines snort in steam across her acres;
As they mark upon the blasted heaven the measure of the land."

"WHAT'S up, old man? Nothing wrong, I hope—no shares gone down alarmingly. Try to look more amiable over it," laughed Gerald Forbes, in his easy fashion, next morning at breakfast, helping himself largely to some grill as he addressed Dudley.

We all looked up. There certainly was a

strange expression on Dudley's face—his eyes were fixed on a reddish, ominous-looking paper—a telegram—in his hand, with a dull, staring, almost stupefied look, and there was a deep line between his eyebrows.

"Wrong? Oh! well, I hope not," he answered, brusquely, as, meeting our inquiring glances, he turned away to the side-table, helping himself to some cold meat; "but it is a confounded bore! If one of our clerks were only to sprain his wrist, I verily believe they would send for me. I am much afraid, however, it will stop my trip with you, Forbes."

"The devil it will! You don't say so! Oh! come, by Jove! you know, that *is* the greatest bore I ever knew!" and Gerald's face expressed genuine dismay.

"Look here, Wyverne, old fellow, there

is nothing serious, I hope, sincerely?" he continued, lowering his voice and coming up behind me to where Dudley still kept hacking away at a spiced round with his back turned. (Was that to conceal his face?)

"Never mind—I'll tell you afterwards; but I am afraid there is the very devil of a row," answered the other, in a hoarse, agitated whisper, which I caught. "Get out your dog-cart quietly, Gerald. I *must* catch this train, and be on the spot at once—it looks uncommonly ugly; and if it be as I suspect——"

"I'll have it round in eight minutes, and take you myself; but, Wyverne, what in the name of all that is sudden are you afraid of?"

"A regular smash!" was the low answer, and I fancied by its stern utterance that he was trying to compose himself under an excitement of no usual nature. A few minutes later we ladies were all in the morning-room when Dudley entered. "Good-bye, Mrs. Forbes. I am afraid I must run away from you this morning," he said, with a smile, and his usual self-possession. "We business men, you see, can never call our time our own; and this is a case of duty before pleasure."

Regrets and protestations from all the ladies of the Forbes family were speedily cut short by the grating of the dog-cart's wheels before the door. Dudley took my hand to say good-bye; the corners of his mouth twitched slightly as I looked up anxiously in his face—the next moment he was gone.

When I arrived home that day, I was met by Nora, who held out a letter with delight.

"It is from Sophy," said the child, "I

know it is: open it quick, and see if she has sent me anything. Aunt Emily would not; for she said you were so queer, you might be angry."

"Am I queer, dear?" I answered, kissing the little traitress, and taking up the envelope which had my name written in Sophia's handwriting, but the rest of the address dashed off in John's large scrawl.

"Well, by-and-by, little one, I will see what it says. There is no such violent hurry."

And by-and-by, accordingly, in my own room, when I had taken off my travelling dress, I sat down to the luxury of enjoying a chat with Sophia, and opened her letter, as I always opened the epistles of my sisters, with an anticipation of enjoyment.

There was a sheet from John, evidently written hurriedly, from the black dashes and ink-spots which besmeared it, but putting this aside as of less consequence, I turned to Sophia's.

"Grove House, Montreal.

"My Dearest Queenie,

"Here am I, seated in my own especial little study (boudoir *you* might call it, only that gives an idea of lolling which does not suit *me*),—prepared to send you as full an account as a pinched, spare half-hour will allow, of my experiences *en route*, and my sensations in the actual 'statu quo.' Of my experiences during the *sea* voyage, indeed, I shall say but little. Memory itself, turning livid at the thought of those heaving heights of water; which, by-the-way, made one think what a decidedly questionable benefit Neptune's wall must have been to Troy, unless the material in former ages was gifted with the superior qualification of 'aqua *firma*.'

"'White waves rising high,' may be all very delightful to those who are indifferent to a proper equilibrium, and whose gastronomic faculties are quite unassailable—but —alas!—I only hope John was imbued with a just sense of all I underwent for his sake. I was nearly repaid, however, for my hardships, by the magnificent beauty of the scenery up the St. Lawrence, which made me keenly regret that I had hitherto neglected to cultivate my natural sketching propensities; not an *idle* regret either, since I fully intend to remedy the omission and give the Canadian Winsor and Newton any amount of custom, so you may soon expect to see some evidences of my industry. I will not attempt to mock Nature, by what must necessarily be a most meagre and inadequate description—but proceed at once to home subjects. Imagine then, my agreeable disappointment at being met on the threshold of that home—not by the creature of my quaking imagination; a tall dragoon-like female, with the impassive sternness of a Valkyrie, who had physically flogged John in his infancy, and would mentally flog him in his prime—a nature against which mine bristled already with instinctive armour—but by a calm, motherly being, with whitest of white hair, and kind, bright eyes, who greeted me most softly and affectionately, when I was forcibly torn from her gentle cooings and kissings by the most vigorous hug that I have ever yet experienced, and found myself in the arms of a bouncing black-eyed hoyden, whose jetty tresses and rosy cheeks gave her quite a gipsy air.

" 'Susan, of course,' I exclaimed, as there was no mistaking the likeness to John, though he is not *quite* so handsome; and then I turned to receive another equally warm, though more stately welcome from old Mr. Demeric, who is quite the type of an old gentleman—so courteous, and charmingly old-fashioned. Indeed, I fear they will think me hard and cold, as I feel with puin the inability of my nature to imitate their show of affection with adequate or corresponding warmth; but if custom does make things easy, *I* should have learnt by now to bear being misunderstood! Captain Graham called to see me the other day, but I was out. He seems to have been very intimate here, yet they have never asked him since I came. Queer, is it not? My only friend here, too; but I intend to learn the reason, if feasible. Two dances have they already given in my honour, and, indeed I am (and shall be) going through such a round of dissipation that any *improving* occupations have been quite interrupted; but I shall not allow my time to be so broken into much longer, since there are so many studies I wish to advance in whenever I have leisure.

"Now, dear Queenie, I must stop, as I hear John bawling that the carriage is waiting to take us to a monster pic-nic, an account of which will—when I return—make a good ending for my letter."

Here the letter stopped short.

"So like Sophia," I said to myself, with a half smile, partly of regret that she had not finished it, partly the sort of pitying fondness with which we so often excuse the small weaknesses, and even petty faults of our dear ones, who would almost lose their individuality in our eyes without such lesser traits, from which we cannot disassociate them. "Of course she went to the pic-nic, and forgot to finish this till the mail was just leaving. Now what does this large brother-in-law of mine say for himself?"

And I less eagerly unfolded his evidently hasty missive,—gave a sudden exclamation, as my eyes rested on the first lines, then, for a moment, could not go on, as the words seemed to stand out larger, and danced and swam before my blurred vision, while my heart beat violently. "Railway accident!—Sophia badly hurt!" was all that seemed clear to me; and at once a terrified foreboding, which was indeed far from unnatural, since my poor Davie's death made all such dreadful possibilities seem terribly usual and every-day chances, made me for a moment or two confused, giddy and trembling like a coward. Then I recovered myself, regaining, as I read on, composure, and said fervently, with a great sigh of relief, "Thank God, it is not so bad, after all! So long as those still left are spared, every other trouble seems comparatively of little importance."

"DEAR QUEENIE," (so ran the letter,) "*don't* be alarmed, but we had a rail accident the day before yesterday, and poor Sophia was badly hurt, and wants me to break the news to you, and I hardly know how to do it. I was *awfully* frightened at first, but now I'm so relieved that I'm half mad with delight—in comparison, you know; but it looked bad, and that's the truth! The whole lot of us were coming back in the cars from a wretched picnic, when an infernal good's train ran straight into us, and very nearly sent us all to Kingdom Come. Such a howling crash as it was I never shall forget; and when I got my senses cleared, found myself walking round and round on the grass, and couldn't tell for the life of me how the"—[here came two mighty ink-blots, and a visible erasure]—"how on this earth I got there; however, *then* I hurried myself pretty smart to look after your sister, and found her, poor dear girl, jammed tight under the stoutest old woman in the Dominion, and such a blessed assortment of smashed seats, shrieking women, legs, arms, splinters and crashed window-frames all on the top of each other, as would be memory enough to last a man his life-time. Luckily we were just close by home, so we brought her back, and my mother and sister (who only want sticking-plaster and gossip to set them straight again) and some more wounded.

"Hurrah!—there is old Sawbones—two of them, and they say she is not going to give it up this time, and have just been having a great consultation. Her right foot is rather crushed, and some small bones broken, but is safe to mend. She complains of feeling twisted and doubled up, but they say they'll pull her through, though it may be slow. I'm so glad again, that I don't know what I'm writing; but they will hardly let me see her; and last night I spent in the passage. If only you were here! Could you not come out by next steamer to nurse her, like a dear girl? Do! I'll meet you anywhere. If you had just only seen the sight, with two engines atop of each other, like fighting bears, and the line of cars like wriggling snakes behind.

Providence saved us all except our driver and two stokers, who were stone dead, poor fellows! I thought the guard would come right again; but instead of that he went to heaven last night—we ought to be truly thankful it was none of us. The mail is going, so must finish up; and don't worry, for you're a sensible girl; and it might be ten times worse.

"Your affectionate brother,

"JOHN DEMERIC."

The amount of sympathy and unexpected kindness on the part of my usually so stern uncle which this news evoked, made me in my gratitude feel ashamed of the fears I had had when looking forward to being entirely dependent upon him and my aunt. His own grief at the loss of the bright boy who had seemed sent to him as his very own to gladden his childless hearth, had, perhaps, for the first time, opened his heart to a sympathy with the sorrows and griefs around him. He no longer looked upon us sisters as mere units among the vast number of womankind with which it had pleased Providence for mysterious and inscrutable purposes to cumber the earth—[it might be as other trials and afflictions were sent to mankind, to be borne with patience, if possible, as chastisements which wisely prevented perfect contentment here below]—now, on the contrary, we were sharers in his grief, and therefore drawn into fellowship with him. Yet, even knowing this, I was considerably surprised when, a little while after, hearing of Sophy's illness, he observed in a meditative manner,

"After all, if one could have foreseen all this, it is certainly a pity you did not go out with Sophia. Feels lonely, poor thing, I daresay; and John Demeric is good-hearted enough, but soft—very soft."

The mysterious nature of Dudley Wyverne's sudden recall to his business, and the fears I had heard him express had been banished from my mind for the moment, when they were suddenly renewed the following morning by Uncle Alick, who, giving a short whistle and then a peculiar grunt to himself, as he studied the newspaper, observed to me, looking over its edge,

"Nice fix this will be for our friend Master Wyverne. Everitt & Everitt—that's the firm he is junior in, isn't it? Humph! thought as much. By gad! it looks very like suicide of Everitt's. Read it for yourself;" and he tossed me the paper as he left the room.

My eyes travelled rapidly over the

columns, then were arrested by the following paragraph:

"FRIGHTFULLY SUDDEN DEATH OF A FELLOW-TOWNSMAN.—Early yesterday morning several of the leading inhabitants of our town, more especially those forming the commercial portion of our community, were startled by the sudden and unexpected intelligence of the death of Mr. Thos. Everitt, well-known as the principal partner of one of our leading firms in Z——. It is stated that the immediate circle of friends and relatives belonging to the deceased gentleman had been aware for some time past that he had been suffering from symptoms of a physically painful nature; but they were thrown none the less into consternation on receiving news of the appallingly sudden nature of his demise. It is not our place to give circulation in these columns to rumours of a wide-spread nature relating to this unhappy event, which are nevertheless whispered on every hand; but we may at least hope sincerely to find them contradicted, since they affect so seriously, not only the credit of this firm, but would also seem to threaten with ruin the prospects of all who have a share in it."

"Ruined!—Dudley ruined!" I exclaimed, looking blankly at the paper; and then laying it calmly down, as one who could expect nothing better from adverse fate, and felt inclined, in a spirit of hardened recklessness, to dare it to the worst.

"I seem to be a very Jonah, bringing evil on all connected with me," I said in bitterness of spirit. "No use in fighting against my fate. I am born under an evil star, and trouble seems to come to all those who care for me."

Soon all the circumstances became fully known, and two or three days later Uncle Alick, who had gone to sit on the Bench, brought back full particulars, which he had learnt from his brother magistrates.

"Heard all about that Mr. Everitt's suicide," he remarked abruptly that evening, with his back to the fire and his eyes on the ceiling; while my aunt and I, seated near the lamp, looked up from our respective books. "They were all talking about it to-day."

"Heard!—did you? Now, Alick, do sit down and tell us comfortably all about it," cried Aunt Emily volubly, with eager coaxingness, laying aside her novel, and patting an absurdly tiny chair with her long fingers.

"*Sit!—sit!*—No, thankee; haven't the slightest intention. The man took an overdose of laudanum, that's all."

Then, as my aunt, fearing the disappointment of her curiosity, still sought to worry out the details by reiterated questions, he at length informed us all he knew; viz., that the firm of Everitt and Everitt was now known to be almost irretrievably ruined. It seemed as if the principal partner, a weak, but well-principled man, had lost his own clear judgment lately, owing to ill health, and had been accustomed to rely for some time previously on Dudley Wyverne's advice. This had by no means pleased the younger

Everitt brother, "a headstrong fool," as Uncle Alick politely designated him, who had bitterly resented the interference of his junior. A protracted strike in the winter, when they had held out against their workmen, contrary to Dudley's earnest advice, and the example of other masters, had been a severe blow; and it seemed that they had afterwards tried to right themselves by hurrying into speculations during a period of Dudley's absence, and without his knowledge.

"There is no use trying to explain it all to you," he continued. "When women try to meddle in business matters, it generally *is* a precious muddle. However, the long and the short of the matter is that they're SMASHED. Horse, Foot, and Dragoons!—shouldn't think they'll manage to save much out of the fire. I saw Forbes for a moment with his head out of the train, very full of the whole affair, and pitying Wyverne."

"But surely Mr. Wyverne won't be utterly ruined?" said I, secretly hoping to elicit something which might cheer my drooping hopes. Something which might make me feel less utterly disspirited as to the sudden blow which had befallen the man whom I had but lately so gladly known to be (yet had blushed even in thought to call) my lover. "If it was not his fault, he will be certain to get another place, I should suppose; and Mr. Wyverne is not a man to give way at the first blow," I somewhat proudly added.

"Don't know, I'm sure. Rather fancy it will be looked upon as a great disgrace to all concerned in it. Poor devil, it is hard upon him, certainly! They say he is the only one who showed brains in the matter; still, he will hardly get clear out of it."

A disgrace! I was hotly indignant at the bare suggestion, but had to chafe my soul in silence. How I loathed the very name of Everitt!—though till now I had hardly ever heard it mentioned in my life. What right had they to drag down Dudley Wyverne, of all men in the world the most honourable, the most conscientious, proudest, truest—ah! what was he not?—to drag him down into the whirlpool?

Now I knew what I had not known before—knew that I could never give him up as I had given up all thoughts of being more than a friend to Harvey Graham. Six days ago, at Longfield, I had been self-doubting, trembling, shrinking away from the old memories, fearful of laying up others which should prove as bitter. The very fact of his being rich made me distrustful of my own feelings for Dudley—now they were put to the test, and I felt they were as true as steel, felt in my folly almost a joy at the calamity which had made it so imperative upon me to give my whole heart—everything—to the man whose good fortune had deserted him. Now at last I knew what it would cost me never to see him again, or to see him other than when last we met. I would break stones on the road gladly, if only I could see him pass by sometimes; would toil, pinch, work, starve with him, if he did but ask it! But what need to think of such a desperate pass as that? He would rally—I knew it! With his courage, cleverness, and perseverance, he could do anything; and then—and then——

Ah! yes, what then? If I had but foreseen all!

We watched very eagerly for the arrival of the next Canadian mail; still more eagerly did we open the expected bulletin from John, which we had encouraged each other to believe would contain accounts of our distant invalid's rapid progress to recovery; therefore our hopes were somewhat dashed when we had at last mastered its rather confused and incoherent contents. Sophia was better, certainly; that much was satisfactorily plain; but the "how much better" was not clear enough to content us. It seemed that she was low, nervous, and most desponding; and though the small bones which had been fractured in the foot were uniting favourably, yet there seemed to have been a shock to her whole system, which the doctors feared might have a long, though they trusted not a lasting, effect. John ended by an earnest, almost entreating, appeal to me to come out and spend the summer with them, which in its schoolboy eagerness irresistibly reminded me of his well-known ways—how I knew them of old! But what touched me more than all he could say was a little slip of thin blue paper, on which was feebly scrawled, in pencil,

"DEAREST QUEENIE,—Won't you come, if you can, to

"Yours ever,

"SOPHY."

There was a silence of a few moments amongst us after the last words had been read. My mind was full of a sudden resolve which I was rapidly maturing. They seemed at a loss to know whether to take the matter cheerfully, or in a desponding view. My uncle hemmed, cleared his throat, and looked sternly out of the window, with his hands in his pockets. Aunt Emily was the first to speak, which she did with a great sigh, and an air of conscious martyrdom.

"Oh, dear! oh, dear! Poor unfortunate Sophia! Something always was certain to happen to her which never happened to other people. She always *was* peculiar. And now I suppose we shall all be in misery about her the whole summer. And, indeed, we may just as well make up our minds at once to her being an invalid all her life—*that* I plainly foresee!"

"You do?" said Uncle Alick calmly, with preternatural mildness.

"Yes, Alick—plainly! That unlucky marriage of hers!—what better could one expect from it? I *never* liked it from the first. Not that I said anything. My advice, of course, was certain not to be taken."

"You are just a little late now, at all events."

"And as to this wild idea of theirs, it is

the most outrageous one I ever heard of," continued my aunt, straightening herself stiffly as she proceeded, all unheeding the treacherous quiet of the atmosphere. "As if I should dream of letting Queenie out of my own care! Most certainly not!"

"Oh! you would not?"

"No!" with tight lips and prim emphasis. "The most preposterous, absurd idea!—but just like Sophia!"

"Well, all I can say is that I consider it the most natural, and right, and proper suggestion they could make," suddenly almost bellowed Mr. Burke, turning upon her with accumulated wrath, and hotly determined on his own course of action, now that she had taken the false step of attempting to dictate in what he considered his own especial field of jurisdiction.

Then, while his wife stared aghast at

the unexpectedly startling turn of affairs, he, spluttering and reddening in anger, hurled a thundering declamation against her hard-hearted unfeelingness, which was exactly what (and nothing better) you might always expect from every woman, when she was put to the test; and, for his part, he would wash his hands of the whole affair; though, at the same time (with slight inconsistency), he declared that he, and he alone, had the control of my actions, and that he —if no one else—would at least tell me that I ought to consider my sick sister, and give up my own pleasure for her; if, indeed, such a sacrifice could be expected from one of a sex who first and foremost always considered themselves. That was his say, and he had said it; though he would not have himself considered as tyrannical by *forcing* me to go.

"No force is necessary," I quietly answered, when the force of his rhetoric was spent. "I have been wishing that I could go ever since her first letter came, but was afraid you would not like it. Now I *must* go."

"Wishing to go, have you? Then why, by all that's absurd and ridiculous, could you not say so ten minutes ago, instead of letting me waste my breath?"

So this, to me, great question was thus settled, and one of my dreams of making long voyages at last to be realized, though mournfully so, and I would be on my way to Canada by the very next steamer that started from Londonderry.

For the next few days I was busily employed packing, in making all my arrangements, and leaving all my parish or other duties in as satisfactory a state as possible; while short, hasty letters had to be dashed off to Nellie, and to other relatives and friends. Uncle Alick watched all these processes of departure with good-humour, while Aunt Emily, on the contrary, suddenly found herself a prey to neuralgia, headaches, and various slight indispositions, which principally took the form of a strange and unaccountable buzzing "in the right—no, the left side of her head."

Entering the room one morning, and addressing me over her shoulder, she said, coldly, with a deep sigh,

"Your uncle wishes you to go and call on Mrs. Lascelles this afternoon. You had better order the carriage."

"On Mrs. Lascelles? Is there any particular reason, for I shall be really so very, very busy to-day?"

"Oh! no reason at all, that *I* know of. I believe he has heard of some officer's wife going out to that horrid country, and that Mrs. Lascelles can tell you all about her. Not that I know anything about the matter; and since you are to be allowed to go there without me to look after you, I suppose I need hardly make my poor head worse to-day about it." Then having delivered this shot rather bitterly, she stalked out again, gaunt and grim as ever, leaving the door wide open, to mark her displeasure.

The task was not pleasant, since I had never quite got over my old feelings of dislike to the now widowed Mrs. Lascelles, though she had lately found it convenient to pay Ballymore frequent visits, and give us the benefit of all her most taking, pretty ways, which were somehow thrown away upon the criticising spinsters and carping matrons of Maghrenagh—where, since poor Joe Lascelles' death, she had come to live. These had rigid second-rate ideas on the subject of widows'-weeds, and were fond of discussing all stray crumbs of gossip they could glean concerning "the life she had led" her deceased husband—pitying the unknown but certain future successor to that proto-martyr, over the high teas and homely gatherings of that small and most quietly behaved of fishy, salt-smelling sea-side towns.

As I drove alone into Maghrenagh that afternoon I had ample time for reflection, and no want of things to think about—not cheerful, some of them, yet I persisted in taking the sunniest view I could of them.

What if Sophia were ill? Was I not going out purposely to nurse her into rude health again?—and of course I should succeed; and I should see her again, which otherwise I could not have hoped to do for long months. My guardian was as gruffly amiable as a lately fed lion, while Aunt Emily's anger at her authority being set aside would last only for a time, and disappear with the mysterious humming and buzzing in her head which accompanied it.

There *was* one prospect, certainly, which I did not like to think of, and which in itself would have deterred me from going had it not been a duty to do so. Meeting Harvey Graham could only re-open a recent wound. Despite our changed feelings it would only be unpleasant, if not absolutely painful to both of us; yet what choice had I? Well, Canada was wide, and his regiment might soon be ordered elsewhere. If not, I must bear the strangely-mixed pain. Then I should come home again and find Dudley as kind and true as ever, once more working his way forward towards success; should care for him ten thousand times more than in his rich days, while I dared trust him blindly to be true to me.

What was he doing now, I wondered; and as the carriage rolled along between dark bog-ditches on either side full of black peat-water, I looked over the cold, sterile surface of turf and heather which lay for half a mile around, then away beyond over the pale spring green of the land stretching flatly towards Z——. He was there. And dreaming and imagining fondly half of the present and his thoughts (perhaps, even in the midst of his troubles, of me), half of a bright future, I hardly knew when we had driven into a more cheerful-looking country and arrived at Mrs. Lascelles' house. This was a pretty villa with large balconies—too close to the road, but with pleasure-grounds behind running down to the sea, which here crept slowly into a tiny bay, shallow and sandy, like all the coast around.

Mrs. Lascelles had just gone into the garden, said the servant, in answer to my inquiries. I should find her, he believed, sitting outside the window.

Having seen her, though not with pleasure, yet rather often lately, since, as I said, she found it convenient in her enforced solitude to show a great liking for our society (perhaps because ours was the only large country house within reach, and that she would not condescend to the Maghrenagh level), I thought I might venture to find her myself, and then hurry home as soon as possible; so I stepped out of her drawing-room window on to the lawn, and proceeded to follow the servant's directions.

She was nowhere to be seen near the house, though a novel of Victor Hugo's and a shawl lay on the short grass; so, turning down a side-walk, I decided she was on the beach; then, fancying I heard voices in front of me, I hurried on under low, pale-green beech branches. Suddenly, as I turned a corner past thick laurels and rhododendrons, I stopped dead short, and involuntarily sprang back again. What had I seen? *Who*—who was that man with his back to me, leaning against the pillar of a rustic summer-house, covered with creepers, which stood back from the walk, half-hidden by the bushes which sheltered me—bending down his head, low, tenderly, to a woman's slight figure in deep mourning, whose face was hidden on his arm? *It was he—Dudley Wyverne!* Though I could not see his face, I should have known him amongst ten thousand. Then I turned sick and faint, while my heart beat so violently that its throbs seemed to fill my ears with a dizzy sound—or what noise was it? It seemed to me they must hear its wild beats, though I pressed both hands tightly, as if to keep it still. I was so close to them too—so close.

She was half sitting, half lying on the bench, with her black draperies of mourning weeds trailing on the ground—had just thrown herself down there beside him as he stood over her—so I knew with the quick, divining instinct of mad jealousy—thrown herself down with both hands clasped on his arm, and was sobbing, with her fair, false face buried against his sleeve. Oh! I could see it all, though that branch with freshly-opening, tender beech-leaves would sway gently against my face, as if to hide them!—hear them too, for all that surging sound in my ears.

"They made me marry him—indeed they did," she was sobbing; "but I never could bear him—never. And now that I am free it is all yours, Dudley, is it not? Indeed, indeed, I never cared for one of them but you! People were wicked enough to talk, but you are too true-hearted to believe them."

"I believed in you once," he broke in; and his voice sounded deeper than usual to my longing, dreading ears. "Six years ago, in my boyish folly—but your conception of a man's ideas of honour must be strange, or you would not think it so easy to take *now* what I could not get *then*."

She raised her head and threw herself backward, looking in his face, but still clutching his arm tightly with white, soft fingers.

"We were both so poor then—so *miser-*

ably poor!" she gasped, in broken, appealing little sentences, while her blue eyes, like wet gentians, swimmingly sought his. "And they spoke harshly to me, Dudley; but it is all mine now—yours, I mean," and her head, with its fair, yellow plaits, drooped again. (But not so low that I could not but catch every silvery inflection of her soft, faltering voice as she pleaded.) "And you have forgiven the wrong I did you—have you not? For I suffered so much—and now things are so different; and—" her voice died away.

Then I heard Dudley slowly answer, as he drew himself up straighter, and looked away out seawards.

"Yes, I forgave you long ago; and, as you say yourself, things are different now."

I heard no more, for next I found myself noiselessly, rapidly, breathlessly gliding back under the beech-trees towards the house. Ringing the bell in the drawing-room, a room crowded with flowers, heavy with scent, full of soft couches, and of useless but lovely trifles—everything that could appeal to the senses—I said calmly to the servant,

"I think Mrs. Lascelles must have gone some distance, as she has not come back to her seat. I am rather hurried, so will you say I am sorry I can neither wait nor go to look for her, but I shall write her a note instead?"

Then I was in the carriage rolling homewards, stunned, miserable, bewildered, not knowing what to think nor what to believe in. Nothing to support me on every side save reeds that bent and broke; and I had thought them strong-rooted trees!

I did not allow myself to be misled by

any false glimmer of hope. He could not have been absent from business and with her at such a time but for one reason—that, being ruined, "he had forgiven her; and things were different!"

The solid foundations on which I had so securely built seemed now all crumbling, cracking, breaking away beneath my feet. But it must be my own fault, in some hidden way, which I tried dumbly to fathom, but could not—mine only that all these whom I had so trusted in, could not be true to me even if they would.

CHAPTER V.

A NOISE OF MANY WATERS.

"Ships that pass in the night, and speak each other in passing,
Only a signal shown and a distant voice in the darkness;
So on the ocean of life we pass and speak one another,
Only a look and a voice, then darkness again and a silence."

OUT at sea in the middle of the Atlantic. It is a bright, breezy morning, and the sun is shining upon miles and miles of deep, heaving, rolling, surging green water; sunning the white decks of a long, narrow steamer, whose apparent length compared with her breadth makes her resemble a race-horse as, while pressing forward to still distant shores, she cleaves her way at twelve knots an hour with all the speed which her powerful engines can give her; warming pleasantly too a figure in a tight-fitting serge dress, proof against spray and wind, which was looking over the ship's side.

This was the fifth day of my life at sea; but during the last two it had blown so hard that but few of the ladies left their cabins, even to venture into the comfortable saloon; and, among the sixty passengers whom chance had crowded together into this floating hotel, but four and the Captain had strength of mind and body to bear them through the courses of a well-appointed dinner.

It is five minutes past twelve now, at which hour the lunch-bell, gave the signal for a general rush below stairs, leaving me the only passenger on deck, for I had begged Mrs. Winthrop, who was taking charge of me, to let me stay behind. Then I look round cautiously, pull a letter from its hiding-place in the front of my dress, but, before unfolding it, lean my head on my hand, to go in memory back again to the few days spent at home before starting.

With a quick thrill of anger I recalled Mrs. Lascelles' malicious congratulations on my journey, when she had, with apparent kindness, driven over to tell us that a Mrs. Winthrop, an old school-friend of hers, was going out with her husband and sister in the same vessel as myself; and the cold, sneering smile, which had come across her pretty face as she observed that I should meet Captain Graham among other friends out there, adding that, "Mr. Wyverne had seemed so surprised on hearing of my voyage, till she had reminded him what attractions Montreal could offer me."

How I hated her with an impotent hatred, powerless to defend myself against her sharp, small poisoned shafts—but how pretty she had looked! Then she was gone, and next morning had come a letter, the very letter which now is lying under my hand, and which once more I read and look at, and re-read again, as if hoping to find something new, some chance loophole to admit a ray of light, some word which might possibly bear another meaning, some expression of tenderness which I might perchance have overlooked, misinterpreted.

But there is no change in those few lines, written firmly and blackly, as if by a man whose mind is made up, and who forthwith rushes into action.

"My dear Miss Demeric,"—(I smile a little sadly to myself, for I used to be something more than merely Miss Demeric, to him at least.)—"You must have heard, like all my other friends, of my change of fortune, which obliges me once more in life to begin on the lowest step of the ladder. I make no comments upon what has caused this, but I cannot help feeling that the change may oblige me to abandon hopes and wishes formed under happier circumstances. A half unwilling hearing which you gave me not long ago, when I had more than merely poverty to offer, cannot trammel you now; but lest, in your great goodness to me, you should let my words trouble you, I felt it right and necessary to say this. I shall be in your neighbourhood again, so I shall hope to see you before leaving Z——, which I shall probably do for a short time; and believe me to remain, under all circumstances,

"Your sincere friend,

"Dudley Wyverne."

But he had never come. Probably Mrs. Lascelles had prevented him, since she seemed to have a slight inkling of how matters had stood between us.

"Better not," thought I to myself, "for explanations, after what I had seen and heard, would be as painful as useless. Better not."

But I thought again of how every night had been one long nightmare to me since I had witnessed their fond meeting in the summer-house; every morning how I had awakened with the first chirp of a bird in the ivy round my window, only to feel a vague sense of misery; then, remembering fully all my trouble, would turn again, and vainly try by closing my eyes to shut out memory.

How pleasant it is to awaken with a drowsy foretaste of joy on the earliest arousing of one's senses; how painful when the first grey beams of ghostly light creep through, only to bring one more long day of dragging despondency!

Then at last I aroused myself with an effort, and try to watch with interest the foaming green swathes of water fall away from the ship's side, wondering idly to myself whether Harvey Graham's thoughts on crossing last year were at all like mine. Probably not; for love in a man's mind, after the fever-fit is over, has only a part amongst other thoughts—it may be a very great part—but still it is only a part; while in a woman's mind (and notably in that of Queenie Demeric, with whose feelings I am the most intimately acquainted) it was the pervading essence, subtly stealing through and permeating the whole. Being greatly in love on a man's part seems like standing on a high mountain-top in the sunlight, with dazzling white clouds stretching beneath him all around in fairy panorama, giving only faint glimpses through the rifts of the glens, nestling villages, or smoky towns lying far below. It is beautiful while it lasts, but he cannot stay long up there among the clouds; by-and-by he comes down again into the work-a-day world, and goes his way too among his bustling fellow-men, remembering with a thrill of pleasure at odd times the enchanted beauty of that cloud-land scenery, but still bending his mind to practical necessities more or less strongly, according to his needs.

A woman, on the other hand, comes down also into the valley, but she brings her clouds with her—their misty vapour may be an invisible accompaniment, but at least she herself is aware of it; and no matter how much she may go about her busiest duties and most pressing occupations, it always surrounds her, interposing its shadowy wall even between her and the things she touches, saturating and pervading heart and mind and work. Give time, however, and of course, like all earthly things, the cloud will lift by degrees, the mist clear and gradually roll away; but there are clouds and clouds, different as those which make the piled white sailing masses on every summer's day a new and beautiful, always changing wonder; rosy from the last good-night kiss of the sinking sun; or purely snowy as those which, to the German poet's glad, fervent eyes, drinking in all beauty, seemed God's white sheep going forth to pasture. Such we may reverently trust and pray our love-cloud may prove to each and all of us—no unhappy, cold, sunless vapour stealing its way into our heart and soul with a deadening chill; yet, even if it should be so, remembering humbly that what is—is best!

The noise of some feet hurrying upstairs again aroused me once more—(they belonged to those passengers who have first satisfied hunger, and seem now vainly seeking some new excitement)—so my cherished letter, my one memento, was suddenly hidden, and I looked up to chat with Major Winthrop as gaily as I can. [I must explain that I had recognised an old acquaintance in him, when he and his wife kindly took charge of me at Derry. Except that his moustaches are, if anything, more bushy than ever, he is nowise changed from the big, honest soldier I met on my first visit to Longfield.]

We, that is, his party of three and myself, have got to know each other very intimately on board ship, since very few of the other passengers are pleasant acquaintances; and so just now we watch a lot of porpoises, or scan the horizon for a passing sail—among the few sights which vary the monotony of our life. Every day our party has seemed to get larger, as fresh faces appeared on deck; and now I turn to smile with my friends at the air of unconcern and not-having-been-at-all-seasick which some very yellow Yankees try to assume as they pace past us. It rather surprises one after being some days at sea to see an apparent stranger walking about; and one wonders at first how he got there.

The afternoon passes monotonously till, at four o'clock, the dinner-bell is rapturously hailed as the principal event of the day. In the evening I played chess in the saloon with Major Winthrop, or else ensconced myself on one of the sofas along the walls, with his wife or sister; pretended to read, but ended by discussing animatedly such congenial topics as our respective dress-makers—my old distaste for such conversation being succeeded by a restless necessity to participate in any talk, however trivial, which banishes sore thoughts awhile.

So the days go on; and though I enjoy my sea-life, the time hangs somewhat on our hands, and I long to be with Sophy, and see her dear prim face again.

How I hated that dense fog which made us lose a day and a half off Newfoundland, and despised the caution which would not allow us to run right through at full speed, sounding the fog-whistle, as used to be the custom. But Mrs. Winthrop complained more loudly, and, turning to our gruff old captain that night at tea, inquired in piteous tones, "whether it was *always* foggy just there, as some one had told her?" To which he replied,

"How the —— should I know? Do you suppose I *live* on the banks?" An answer which elicited looks of well-bred indignation from all of us.

At last—at last! on the evening of the twelfth day we had spent on board, came the welcome sound of "Land right ahead!" and we strained our eyes for hours to see it, although not till next morning were they gladdened by the sight.

Then came the journey up the noble St. Lawrence—the feeling that I was drawing nearer and nearer to friendly faces—Montreal itself one day; then a drive out of town, a bustle of arrival, and, finally, Sophia's arms round my neck, mine round hers, and every one else forgotten in the mutual joy of sisters meeting again.

CHAPTER VI.

WEARIED WITH THE MARCH OF LIFE.

"Oh, my lost love, and my own, own love,
And my love that loved me so!
Is there never a chink in the world above,
Where they listen for words from below?"

"IT is such a lovely evening! you really ought to go out, and not shut yourself up the whole of the day, Queenie dear," said my sister's somewhat quavering, invalid voice, the day after my arrival.

"Go out, when I seem only to have spent a moment with you! Consider how late I slept this morning, too," I replied, brightly, clearing away a small tray from near her sofa and softly arranging the green blinds.

Then I seated myself on a low stool close to her couch, with a large feather fan, and sometimes fanning her poor feverish face, watched how it brightened as we talked; turning occasionally to glance out through the open window under the half-drawn venetians towards a lovely peep of a little lakelet set in green, with a wooded hill rising steeply behind it, and both framed in the branches of two tall maples standing on either side of my narrow view.

"So you say that Susan never really cared for Captain Graham? She looked a bright, fresh girl, I thought, this morning."

As if involuntarily, my fan hid my face one moment from Sophia's too constant gaze of affection.

"No. She is rather a flirt, you know; but really I can't be angry with her, she is so bright and good-humoured. She told me she could not help his liking her—that it was a common complaint—and that she thought Captain Graham was a man who must always be liking somebody."

"Did she refuse him, then?" And my voice sounded slightly sharper, to my own thinking.

"It did not come to that. She grew tired of him, I believe, but at that pic-nic he seemed quite himself again. Since I have been ill, who do you think has been coming here?—and John tells me he really believes Susan likes him better than anyone else, though she says she hates him. He came out a fortnight ago, you know, and has been here constantly."

"Who?"

"Gerald Forbes. Does it not seem strange? What brings him here I can't think, for Susan often sits with me, and John too, and yet he stays on downstairs."

"There he is himself, I verily declare!—walking under the window, and talking to that grave, solemn old doctor of yours." And it seemed to me strangely like old times to peep out and watch Gerald's well-known stooping figure.

"The doctor grave? He is always bright with me. And when did he come?" asks Sophy, rousing up slightly, with a look of surprise, for she had not expected him.

"I saw him two hours ago, coming out of a room on the right of the library," I somewhat incautiously answer.

"That is only a spare bedroom on the ground-floor. John, what brings the doctor to-day? I don't want him, and I shan't see him," she petulantly called out to that individual, who just then entered.

John looks somewhat confused.

"Very well, Sophy, darling! of course you will. I mean—just as you please," he answered, sitting down with a heavy thump, wrinkling his forehead, and rubbing it with one big hand, like a puzzled schoolboy.

"But what did he come for?" she persisted.

John gave a deep sigh.

"My dear girl, how should I know? Oh! however, I believe he came to—to see my father on business, I think." Having so answered, turning away his head ostentatiously, and studying the cornices.

"Your father has been in town all the afternoon; and what was the Doctor doing downstairs in the spare bedroom, then?" asked my sister, sharply, transfixing the back of his big, foolish, but honest, black head with a keen, suspicious glance.

A convulsive movement of John's body,—a sudden crash, and down went poor Sophy's little table, and her pile of pet books. She closed her eyes faintly, all her unstrung nerves jarred by the shock. I looked in reproach, while the unhappy culprit picked himself up from his low seat with a ponderous movement, gave himself a shake, like a large Newfoundland dog, and retreating towards the door, made insane and violent gestures to me, with his fingers on his lips.

"Sophia is not asleep, John," I answered, quietly, but outright. "You are not exactly so soothing in a sick-room as all that." So saying, I go down on my knees to pick up the volumes and scattered flowers.

No answer, but a rattle of the door-handle, and frantic dumb movements of

John's lips, while one thumb keeps jerking towards his wife's unconscious head. I flashed back with my eyes an indignant order to keep quiet; then, in despair at guessing his meaning, observed, with an air of carelessness,

"Suppose you take me out for a few minutes, John; I think I should like some fresh air!"

"Yes, dear; pray go out—it is good for you," said my sister, with affectionate solicitude, unclosing her eyelids for a moment, while John's face beams with a broad gleam of approval of my cunning, and assenting with suspicious eagerness, he closed the door with careful creaks, more irritating to an invalid than any moderate amount of noise, but which only brought an indulgent smile on my sister's pale, suffering features.

Before leaving her, I shook up her pillows tenderly, lingering reluctantly to see if there are no other little loving cares I could show her; then, telling her maid in the next room to watch over her, quit my poor sick one at last; but John was not in the passage. Opening the swing-door which shut off my sister's apartments from the rest of the house, I saw a gentleman at the end of the corridor which ended in a deep window, forming a sort of alcove. He was kneeling with one knee on the window-seat, and looking down towards the glittering tin roofs of the town in the distance; then, hearing the rustle of my dress as I came down the passage, turned eagerly to hold out his hand.

"Mr. Forbes! How glad I am to see you!" I exclaimed with delight, for a familiar face in a strange land is like Friday to Robinson Crusoe. "How strange it seems for you and I to meet out here—does it not?"

"The world is very small, after all, which may be a blessing, considering how few people worth anything it holds," he answered, with a touch of his old cynicism; inviting me by a motion to sit down on the broad window-seat, commanding a view down the small valley.

"So it was to see you that John beckoned me out. He might have spoken plainly; but John is such an absurd, dear, good-hearted fellow," I said, as I seated myself, smiling at my big brother-in-law's clumsy manœuvres.

Gerald had grown odder than ever. He looked furtively at me from under his eyebrows, then out of the window, and abruptly said for all answer, as much to the air as to me,

"I never knew of this dreadful railway

accident till I got out here. You know I started without Wyverne, just two days after you left us at Longfield."

"That must have spoiled the fun of your trip."

"Well, two other old Oxford men came out with me; I had meant to start with them for Ottawa five days ago, but here I am still, you see."

Remembering Sophia's confidential communication, I smiled ever so little.

"You are thinking, *que fais-tu dans cette galère*," he answered quickly; "but, you see, the only people I know here are in this house . . . and a dreadful accident it has been to some of them."

I looked up with surprise at the young man's strange, meaning tone, but he was pulling off some flower-petals from a plant beside him, and would not meet my eyes.

"You don't think that Sophy——" I began, while some alarm crept into my voice.

"No, no; your sister, I hear, is coming round slowly but surely—no, I meant others."

His voice dropped so low at the last words as to be almost unintelligible.

"Others! Why, all the Demerics—my uncle, aunt, John, and Susan—look as blooming as possible. My cousin is pretty—don't you think so?"

"Very—excessively so;" and rising, he leant his arms on the deep window-ledge with more embarrassment than ever: then, after a long pause, continued, in a low voice—"I was greatly shocked to find an old friend of mine had been hurt in that accident. I have come here every day since I learnt it."

"Here! Where? Not to this house, do you mean?"

"Yes. You know it happened only a quarter of a mile from here, and he was carried so far—he will never go further, I fear."

"How terrible!" I said, in an equally low voice, catching the infection of dread in his—a dread we all feel for those who are slipping away from our grasp, our ken; passing from us to the great Unknown Land. "Sophia does not know, does she? How was he hurt?"

"No; they were afraid of the effect on her nerves, as it was only a question of time from the first. It is his spine, poor fellow. The doctor was telling me half an hour ago that his time is nearly run out." Gerald's voice sounded husky. "Such a prime, good fellow as he used to be—don't you think so?"

"How should I know, poor man? I never knew him, did I?" And my voice, though awestruck, could not reflect his genuine feeling for his friend. He looked away, then answered in a very low voice,

"*Yes, you did know him!*"

An exclamation of surprise, suddenly checked by a sharp catch of my breath; a long silence; at last (it seemed after many minutes, during which not a sound was heard, but some faint, distant noises, reaching us through many doors in our secluded corridor)—I touched his coat-sleeve, and hoarsely murmured,

"How did you know that—that——?"

"He told no one else; but I have been sitting up with him several nights, and when he heard you were coming, he seemed to rally—to the surprise of the doctors. Last night he told me for the first time he thought he could not go in peace till he had seen you."

"Does John know?"

"Yes. He asked me to tell you. No one else knows; but only say you will come —it is his one dying wish," and he turned to me in touching entreaty. "He is so much attached to you, Miss Demeric. Surely no woman could be cold enough to refuse—it is the only thing he asks for. Poor old Harvey! he and I are such friends I would do anything on this earth for him now," and his voice broke down; "so, when I found what his mind was set on, I swore to myself that if any begging or praying of mine could move you——"

"I am going, Mr. Forbes."

"God bless you! It is so good; but I knew you would." And he shook my cold hands. "John is waiting for us."

. . . . . .

Downstairs there is a pleasant room on the ground-floor—the verandah which runs outside it, covered with Virginian creepers, keeps it cool in this hot summer weather, and dark—alas! soon to be still darker to brave, patient eyes, over whose gaze the deepest of all shadows—the shadow of another world—is creeping. There are signs of loving care in all the little sick-room arrangements—a screen partly hides the table on which tumblers, medicines, and phials are carefully arranged—vain weapons, which may now be laid aside, since the struggle is almost over—the battle fought out. Some beautifully soft proof-engravings of holy subjects were on the walls—one, the Sacred Head, crowned with thorns, on whose rapt expression through more than human agony one suffering pair of eyes have rested through many a night of terrible pain; flowers, too, on a tiny table, offerings flung lovingly from the living on the banks to one whose boat is, alas! floating swiftly by, passing into the great Ocean of Eternity.

But I saw none of these as they brought me in and left me—nothing but the low camp-bed and a motionless figure upon it—nothing hardly of that save two living eyes in a face of marble; and as I dropped down upon my knees by his side their look bridged over in one moment days, weeks, and months; and face to face as we had parted—was it minutes or years ago?—the intervening time forgotten, obliterated!—Harvey Graham and I met once more on the borders between the earth of the living and the land of the dead!

"Queenie, Queenie, don't look so, dear. My soldiering is all done, you see, but I am only going home on a very long leave."

He attempted to stroke my hair with one trembling hand, but the effort was too much, and the intense pain brought cold drops on his forehead, though he tried to smile unflinchingly in my eyes.

"Harvey! Oh, it can't be true—it can't! You are too young and strong . . . . and I never knew it till now—never knew it!" I wailed, in my great yearning to keep him back—not to *let* him die; caressing wildly those powerless hands which should never clasp mine strongly as of old, never do their master's bidding any more. "You must not die!—you must not!"

"Hush, darling, hush! I have got my Captain's orders to go, you see. A soldier's first duty is to obey . . . It has been a long march, and tired me out, Queenie; but I am only one man more dropped out of the ranks."

His mouth quivered slightly as he tried to smile; while he looked away from my longing face, upwards, with a momentary pain in his honest, brave blue eyes.

For a moment it seemed hard. He had thought he could lay down gladly the cares and harness of this life, but when stepping over the threshold, my face, which he had hardly dreamed of seeing again, made him turn with a last look—

Then the struggle was over. He was ready and willing for the summons.

"How is Wyverne? You don't mind telling me about that, do you?" he asked, with a kind smile on his pale lips, and a look which tried to banish all shadow of regret. "Mrs. Lascelles wrote to me saying it was all settled; and I was glad of it, for he is a right good fellow."

"There is nothing to tell—nothing."

(Was I wrong? What could I tell him? But dying eyes see often clearly what might be hidden from our grosser, earthier vision.)

"Nothing to tell now, but there may be something one day—is not that it, Queenie?" And no brother could have asked more tenderly.

"No, never;" and my face was buried down on the bed, while I held his hand in both mine close to my cheek. "He will marry her—Mrs. Lascelles," I whispered, with a choking feeling in my throat. "Oh, how can I forgive her?—my fate, my evil genius! First she wrote to you, and made me so miserable—oh, so miserable! And now—and now—what harm have I ever done her that she should do all this to me?"

"Miserable! And yet if I could have helped it you should never have known a moment's pain." . . . (He spoke slowly with painful hesitation) "But I suppose it was natural enough," he resumed. "I was unhappy at first, thinking of you; and then I heard of Wyverne; and your cousin was awfully kind and nice.—It was only a passing thing, dear, and all over some time ago . . . but people must care for some one or other always, I suppose."

It was a necessity with him to do so, that was true; but I answered nothing. Only I smiled rather sadly; but, such as it was, my look seemed to call up a happy expression of peace on his face; for the only doubt which could have disturbed his last moments was laid to rest.

Then I looked out at the evening sky with a sudden pang that to-morrow would be so different! No one, then, on this whole wide earth who would care for me as even this passing human soul still cared.

"It all seems so hard, Harvey,—so cruel! I am very, very tired of it all, and I wish," —my voice sank away into a tired prayer for rest—"oh! *how* I wish I could go now with you!"

"My dear girl! My poor Queenie! Don't let yourself ever despair . . . Be sure there is some work for you to do—some duty or other. Be brave, darling; do what's right, and never mind the rest."

We were both silent. Outside came a low murmur of men's voices from the verandah, where they were waiting, unwilling to disturb our last interview.

"There is one more thing I want to tell you, while I can," he said, breaking the solemn hush in a voice already weaker, with fitful gasps that made my nerves quiver and my hands tremble in the pain of hearing it, and being so useless—so powerless to help. "Mrs. Lascelles, you know—I was able to pay back that money."

"What does it matter now, Harvey? Don't think of it—think of other things."

"I must. Listen, dear, for I owe it all to Wyverne." (Wyverne! That name was sufficient. I listened intently.) "My poor old aunt left me a legacy just about the time I got out here; so I was heartily glad to pay off the money-lender. But it was Wyverne himself all the while—don't you see? . . . . My mind feels wandering." He stopped with a confused look of pain. "I wrote to Forbes to settle it all for me—yes, that was how it came out. Poor Wyverne! He was smashed just then, and this man let all out to Forbes. I little thought, when Wyverne offered to get it for me at such low interest, that it was he himself who was helping me under cover. You will do it, won't you?"

"Do what, dear Harvey? I will do anything on earth you ask me."

"Tell him—*you* can—he is a right good fellow. Say how I thank him; he never thought I should know. You will be happy, Queenie, and I am very glad. You and he—you and he——"

He seemed wandering, and again I raised my head and watched him anxiously as I knelt beside him.

All at once a great change came over his face—what, I knew not. In sudden alarm I turned and had grasped at the nearest bottles, looking rapidly at the labels. He stopped me by a faint, slight gesture.

"Better now," he murmured, and his face brightened with a momentary gleam. "Come here again, dear. Close—so. I want to look in your eyes again. It was all a mistake for you and me to care for each other as we did; but I, for one, would not have had it different. Forgive me all the pain I gave you. Forgive everything else. Queenie! Queenie! when next we meet we shall understand each other better. We *shall* meet." And a look of great trust and happiness came over his face as he seemed to look into a distance hidden from me. "It has been hard sometimes; never once *too* hard. Remember that always. I am ready now—ready!"

What was that strange brightness over his features? But I could not call—I could not turn—could hardly breathe, lest I should lose one faint word, while his eyes held mine in a spell of fond, dimming, but oh! surely not—not *dying* love!

"I can hardly see your eyes, Queenie.

How dark! Has the sun set? Yes, Lord, I am ready . . . going home . . . home."

A cry—a sharp, bitter woman's cry, which startled two watchers outside. They hurried in and looked, and lifted a woman's fainting, motionless figure, fallen down on the floor in a lifeless heap, but whose life was only suspended, not extinct; while he, my first love, whom I had once so loved, was far away, never to return.

His sun had set.

CHAPTER VII.

OVER THE SEA AND FAR AWAY.

"Yet how grand is the winter! How spotless the snow is, and perfect!
By the window she sat with her work, and looked on a landscape
White as the great white sheet that Peter saw in his vision,
By the four corners let down, and descending out of the heavens,
Covered with snow were the forests of pine, and the fields, and the meadows."

THE summer has passed; the Canadian autumn, too, with all its glowing glories of fading red and crimson and yellow coverings; gorgeous maples, once exulting in the changing beauty of their dying garments, now stripped and bare, except, it may be, where a light covering of snow rests on the upper side of their naked branches, for the winter has come, and yet I am still at Montreal.

It is a bright morning in November. Outside one sees only great sweeps of powdery, glistening snow, broken here and there by dark masses of hemlock or spruce, which seem grandly to resist the power of the bitter cold, but whose great, green, flat-spread branches are flaked here and there by touches of pure white spray, from which the wind of the early morning has not quite freed their broad fans; while I can see the steel-like frozen surface of the lake from where I sit, and the hill beyond, down which many a toboggin has already rushed in perilous shoots, or fortunate, wild, exciting career.

It is a glorious winter—a true Canadian winter; and despite cold, and frost-bites, and drawbacks, who is there on earth who will not sing its praises?

We womankind were all seated this morning in my aunt's own morning-room at Grove House. Hers, however, was no silken-lined nutshell of a boudoir, such as my soul used to revel in, heavy with scent, where every footfall sank dumbly into soft carpets, and each low chair seemed more enervating than the other; for despite the gentle refinement in Mrs. Demeric's serene if rather worn face, and graceful, small person, no one could imagine her merely luxurious—an effete lady, fed on cream and sweetbreads; and rooms reflect their owners. No, it is bright, warm, and looks as if it were always lived in; double windows and a large stove help us to admire the snow without with warm, serene composure; water-colours of Canadian scenes, and large photographs of absent friends, almost cover the walls; instead of flowers, bright, stained, feathery pampas grasses adorn vases on the tables, which are also littered all over with pretty Indian nick-nacks, carved canoes or embroidered work-bags; while, as if to give colour to the whole picture, we are all stitching away busily at piles of scarlet flannel, of which a great bale lies on the floor beside us, strongly suggestive of Christmas times and poor, shivering children.

"There goes my boy's shirt—No. 3! All my brains have run down, I declare, into my finger-tips. Who would ever have thought at home mother, (I mean at Ballymore), that I should take to sewing."

And Sophia, happier and more placid than ever she looked before, if still with an appearance in her face of being always an invalid, gives a deprecatory, almost self-depreciating shrug. A queer little answering smile lurks round the corners of "the mother's" lips, as we fondly call her; while her scissors run swiftly down a long, red seam; for till lately Sophia's shirts have been made upon what we silently imagine to be a theory of her own, being cut straight up and down, guiltless of sleeves, or with those useful appendages put wrong side foremost.

"If reading makes your head ache, childie, why, just wait patiently till it does not," she sagely observes; and then, putting her dear old white head on one side, seems to consider the flannel deeply, with a doubtful look in her bright eyes; while seams and gussets, hems and bands, are evidently dancing in chaos through her brain. Then, having solved the silent problem, she looks up sweetly with a relieved air to add, "I think I am a most fortunate old woman to get one such a useful daughter, when my other is running away from me. I only wish I could always keep my Queenie, too."

Both of us sisters glance up at her affectionately as she sits there, looking always calm and happy, with her snowy hair, and quick, bird-like, bright eyes; dressed in warm woollen grey (the colour she always wears, whether her gown be silk or satin, or only, as now, a plain one for simple morning wear.)

"How little can one foresee how events will turn out," thought I to myself, as moving nearer the window, I sewed busily, leaving the others to talk together round the stove. "In the first place, no one ever imagined Sophy would marry; and then to live in

Canada, with the prospect of being always rather an invalid all her life, would have seemed truly a most dismal future!—yet here she is, happier, perhaps, than any of us, with Aunt Susan as the kindest of mothers, and John and his father studying all her wishes. She seems changing so completely, too, under their kindness, all the old, little, rough excrescences of her nature softening down; while even the want of strength has quieted the vague, craving restlessness which used to fret her. Yes, Sophia will be happier here than ever she could have been at Ballymore—no doubt of that. Except for the pleasure it gives her, I might as well be in Ireland, for she is growing fonder of them all here every day, and of course that is just as it should be. John being first, John's relations ought to come near too. Heigho, Queenie Demeric! About time for you to go elsewhere—no one wants you very specially here."

And thereat I unconsciously sighed, and looked down towards the town, where is a quiet, enclosed spot that I wot of; birches, yews, and cypresses wave over it, or stand up now like white funeral plumes, while spreading over the ground below these a thick, pure, snow covering undulates gently and lovingly over the beds of the silent sleepers beneath. There is a cross under the birches there, small, but broad and massive in shape, which comrades have erected to the memory of a favourite brother-officer, a bright, joyous spirit, if sometimes weak and wavering, yet always kind and generous.

But the mother's eyes were upon me with a look of affectionate solicitude, and, becoming all at once aware of this, I started, pricked my fingers, worked on nevertheless, but by and by fell to thinking on and on again.

I was not unhappy—far from it; rather I had at last learned to bow my stubborn will to a higher one, and was accepting thankfully the tranquil course of every-day life, which brought so little now to disturb me. But still, not yet subdued, not yet quite satisfied, there was the human craving for some one—something to whom I should be necessary, essential, or even in some way or other useful. I had been so formerly to both my sisters, while our road in life was the same, but now our pathways had diverged; and what a thick growth of new ties, interests, and loving associations were springing up under their pleasant hedgerows, which I, as an outsider beyond the fence, and following my own road to vague, unknown fields, could not look at closely, like them, with quite as glad and loving eyes.

There were my guardians. True. But though I trusted I had now learnt a little of the great lesson of bearing and forbearing, if at the cost of sharp teaching, yet there, too, Nora was their child, and the only one their hearts had room for. Even so, was I worse off than so many other single ones who seem to stray aimlessly among happier social groups, where is no set place for them, no room made ready and awaiting such, like the prophet's chamber on the wall?

But is there any human soul whom no one wants? Again my work was put down on my lap. It was the same question I had been asking myself night after night, as I looked out from my warm, comfortable bedroom, on the pure white plain stretching far away beneath the starlit sky, and at the lights of the town gleaming in the distance. And always the same answer came back till it grew a conviction—came back in the words of a song I used to sing at home in summer evenings, in former restless, sometimes deliriously joyful,—were they happier?—days.

> "Each one has some work to do, some duty to fulfil.
> The winds that blow, the flowers that grow,
> The waters never still."

If one can't be first, why, swallow one's pride and be second. If one is not absolutely wanted by some one, one is wanted for something—else why were we put on God's earth? Nothing is purposeless . . . but ah! how to find out what *is* that work, for at times it may lie so close at hand that we overlook it? Only, if possible, I shall not be a solitary star, wandering mournfully among constellations. Each one may be the nucleus of a group of such shining souls, to whom they shall be necessary, no matter in how small a degree!

The kindness of the whole Demeric family had been constant ever since my arrival. It was as if all the inmates of the house had opened their arms to receive me, and Sophia and I seemed, to my fancy, to nestle ourselves in the soft down of gentle words and kindly ways which lined our present life, like half-fledged birds restored to a nest, who had almost forgotten, in their lonely time outside, how pleasant was the warmth and maternal brooding care they used to know!

"Does not Aunt Susan make you sometimes feel as if you were a child again, with mamma looking after you?" I once asked Sophy, in my gratitude, and she had agreed with me.

Gerald Forbes also had been, since that dark evening after my arrival, a firm, if a silent friend, which might, perhaps, have had a mysterious connection with the warmth and affection which my cousin Susan vouchsafed to me when that gentleman left us during two months for his projected tour round the principal towns and up the river. She, too, had cried her black eyes all red and swollen round the lids when poor Harvey's death had made the whole household feel a gloom for want of the frank face and boyish, happy voice they had grown so familiar with: but the summer shower soon dried, and when Gerald Forbes came back again, like a needle to the magnet, she was once more the bright, warm-complexioned, saucy gipsy she used to be.

I was very glad to meet my relations' eager wishes to spend part of the winter with them; and now it had been finally settled that I was only to return to Ireland whenever my aunt and uncle could resign themselves to allow their petted daughter to become Mistress Gerald Forbes.

It was a great day of weeping and rejoicing in Grove House when that gentleman and the young lady first made this small project public; nor could Gerald's plea that, by the laws of compensation, one Demeric ought to be returned to Ireland in place of the one now lost to that bereaved country, much reconcile either my uncle or aunt to parting with their only daughter.

By some one little transparent plea or other the good old people had contrived to reprieve themselves from the final separation month after month, till at last it was gravely agreed in by all parties that, since both Gerald and myself might never again have so good an opportunity of enjoying the sleighing and skating and winter amusements in Canada, it would be a great pity to go back till spring. The wedding was therefore to take place in January, and in March I was to return with the young couple to Ireland—the happy pair most concerned good-humouredly agreeing to appear convinced of the weight of these arguments.

Just now Susan's heart does not appear to be in her sewing, and there is small progress in the flannel-petticoat she is manufacturing for a ragged little lass down in the cottage near the lake—which cabin looked so odd to my unaccustomed eyes, piled round three or four feet deep with bark as it is, to keep out the intense winter cold. Her eyes kept wandering, first to the window, thence to the clock, and then back to the window again.

"Of course you are not thinking of going out this morning, as we are all going down to the Rink in the afternoon?" I observed, maliciously, with a low laugh, not in my own, but in the red flannel sleeve I was sewing.

Susan looked conscious, and was rosier than usual.

"Well, I was thinking," she began slowly, then, as a sop to me warmly continued—"would you like to come out, too? Oh! do come. I believe," with a little laugh—"I believe I *did* promise Gerald to come out this morning about now."

But of course my work was far too important to allow of my entertaining any such proposal. Equally, of course, my cousin was all the more anxious for my company.

"Letters!—letters!—who wants letters!" cried John, entering at this juncture; and then, like the great baby he was, pretended there were none, though we knew it was the day for the Irish mail. Finally, with a flourish, he produced them from his pocket;

and, meanwhile, Gerald and Susan interchanged one of those looks of mutual understanding which are the language of one happy period in life, and the latter departed, to put on mocassins over her strong boots, and wrap herself warmly in sealskin and folds of white woollen cloud, which only left the tip of her nose and her merry eyes visible. There was a letter to me from Nellie, of some half dozen sheets, upon which Sophia also eagerly pounced, so we compromised matters by reading it together —a race in which she outran me, and was impatient to turn over, while I was still lingering enjoyably half-way down the page.

Mrs. Kingston dated from Estcourt, where she and Bob were staying with the Nevilles for the County Races. "Just like old times, except that I have all my own way now. But it seems so odd without you both; not that I pity you, my dears, for you must be having awful fun out in Canada," wrote this nineteenth-century young woman (though without dreaming of using even one of the stops I have here supplied). "We had such a jolly summer wandering about," she continued; after which surprising fact came a bewildering list of names, which we sagely concluded were of places she had seen, in the Tyrol and Switzerland,—all tracks which, if well-beaten, were at least new to my home-bred, little country mouse of a sister. "And here we are again in the old country, just in time for all the balls," ran on the letter. "We have been on a round of visits ever since, and always meet the same set very nearly. The Forbes' are here, and our dear Desmond cousins too—tiresome, tall things! They are so affectionate to me now, and keep flopping after me all day long; but don't I patronise them splendidly, with my nose well up in the air. *They* never inquired after you; but that good old Lady Highlyffe was asking heaps of questions, and sends you her royal and most gracious love.

"Oh! dear, I quite forgot to finish my letter yesterday, and went off to the races instead. To-night I am going to the Race Ball in the most *scrumptious* dress imaginable—heaps of white tulle and satin caught up with bright little birds and green trails; and Bob presented me with such a glorious little diamond Bird of Paradise that sticks up on one side of my head splendidly! I wish you were here to see it. My beloved mother-in-law has just gone off to Ballymore, after inflicting a fortnight of her presence upon us, and I have been bounding like the roebuck or the hart at getting rid of her. Two of

Bob's old brother-officers came to stay with us—great fun both of them, but talk horses and racing sometimes, you know. Oh, what lectures she did give them!—and it made Bob so wild! Then she solemnly presented them each with a pamphlet on the Last Day; she is quite certain it is coming this year, but all the pamphlets give a different date, unfortunately. Well, Bob stopped *that*, and next morning, lo and behold! in came Sir Charles limping to breakfast, sits down beside her very carefully, and gravely consults her as to what can be the matter with his boots, for they *feel so tight*. (I thought she looked guilty). Off he pulled one, and what *do* you think?—into the toe was stuffed a great fat tract called 'Turn or Burn! A Loving Appeal to Sinners!' It seems she often gets her maid to do this, who is an 'earnest spirit,' she says. But the best of all is, that she thinks she has converted Aunt Emily, who has taken a new fit all of a sudden —no less than *doing good!* All the beetles, and butterflies, and seals, and stamps, are put away now. Vick is called a 'cranky little spoilt animal,' and to see Aunt Emily stalking along the lanes, dashing into the cottages, scolding about dirt and untidiness, and then whisking off again, is really worth anything. Uncle Alick never minds—not he! His salmon-fishing was very good, and we all of us know he cares for that more than for anything on earth; he is busy draining *thoroughly* the last field of all, after which I think he may leave Ballymore, for there are no more improvements in that line he could possibly make, and he will be miserable without some big drain to stand over and scold about."

Here the writer branched off into unimportant home details, finishing with an imperious command to me to remember I must return in time to spend the season with her in London, as Sophia had had more than her share of me: and "any amount of loves to all of you from Bella Forbes. She is going to set up an asylum for unmarried young ladies of the county, to be called the Ark of Refuge, and put all her sisters in it, but has not the faintest intention of entering it herself. 'Catch me shut myself up! Not I, my dears! I mean to hang on to the very last thread, and you'll see I'll have as good a chance as any of you bread-and-buttery young things yet.'

"And now for a riddle: Mrs. Lascelles is going to be married! and you may all guess *who* the unfortunate man is—don't I pity him!—just! I shan't tell you the name till next letter, so guess; but you *know him.* I think he must be a fool to do it, but then he wants money."

So it was settled then! At last. My face did not change in the smallest degree as Sophia guessed, wondered, and talked over it. Had I not known it all these weeks? The only strange thing was, why they had kept silent about it until now; then, remembering that Mrs. Lascelles' first year of widowhood had barely elapsed, I wondered no longer. Well, I had had time enough to get accustomed to it, and so I was of course——yet how it stung!

We went to the Rink that afternoon and met a crowd of our acquaintance, and I talked and laughed with all of them till my head ached again; was overpowered with compliments on the progress I was making in skating, and went on still more fast and furiously, with brightened eyes, flushing cheeks—and great sore misery in my heart.

"What splendid spirits you are in, my queen! Why, if you always had that colour, half the girls here would think you a most dangerous rival," said Susan, skating up to rally me with a pleased but surprised laugh, and whispering her remark as I stood in the centre of a gay group. In the evening we drove to a ball given at a house on the other side of the town. My head still throbbed, but I would not stop dancing, for that would entail possible silence, and silence thought, and thought I shrank from almost with fear. The dull pain was always there, sickening, gnawing; it would assert itself soon enough, but while I could, it must be smothered, forced out of sight.

Then we drove home merrily over the silent, snow-covered ground, under a glorious starlit sky, our horses' bells ringing out little peals in the frosty air as the sleigh dashed along.

"Well, I know who talked and danced enough for a dozen to-night," observed John. "What has come over you, Queenie? You were running dark before, I think, but now you mean to take all of us by storm."

"I want to shine brilliantly before I go, like a falling star," I answer as gaily; then, suddenly remembering a conversation long ago, when Dudley Wyverne had spoken of the *étoile qui filait*, I shiver with sick pain, and am silent.

The rest were all talking when I found Gerald goodnaturedly whispering to me,

"You are not quite yourself to-night, I think. Twice or thrice, when you ought to have been happy, I saw you abstracted and dreaming."

"I was excited, and perhaps overtired," I

replied in evasion. "To-morrow you shall see me myself again."

And I kept my word. But that night, tired though I was, how hard it was to sleep! And when sleep at last came to my weary lids, it was with a sense of confused pain through my dreams, which made me turn my head impatiently in half waking, half sleeping, from side to side, instinctively seeking some refuge, while happy memories, whenever they came, only made me wake up with a start, as if I must not escape from my tossing sea of troubles even in that most blessed land of lotos-eating, Lethe-drinking Sleep. Saddest of all it is when the first grey glimmer of morning light stealing in, despite of heavy curtains, only arouses us to a dim, undefined sense of trouble; then comes the fuller remembrance—the sick loathing that another long day is before us, to be lived through—hopeless, grey——

"But I must not be a coward!" I would exclaim, nerving myself to spring up; and the movement seemed to break through my morbid fancies as through spider's filmy threads woven round my head, and I said to myself that no burden was too heavy, if rightly borne—no path so weary, but that a harder and more pitilessly stony one had been trodden before. With the new day came new strength. When does it ever fail, if rightly sought? Work! work! straining our powers for others and with them, and the fresh, healthy air will nerve the tired heart and brain to take interest again in the movement of life. We cannot escape our wholesome grief; try as we may, some time its fires must overtake us, whether to prove us dross or cleanse the metal; but at least we can spare others the sight of our wounds, and not weakly indulge in a false luxury of melancholy. At such times we choose for ourselves whether the blows shall turn the iron to pure steel, or leave us only bruised and battered, crying out against an apparently merciless fate, while the heavens above are as brass, and the earth as iron.

But of all pangs the most humiliating and the keenest to a generous nature is when our idol falls from its shrine, and we cannot escape seeing in its shattered fragments what base earthly clay that is which we once worshipped with such trusting, devoted eyes,—blinded to the truth by the smoke of the incense and dazzle of the lights offered fondly by our own hands before its altar.

With my ideal, my first love, it had been different. Litle by little I had recognised that it was not so much himself, however kind and loveable, but rather my own thoughts, my own ideas of perfection, which I had imagined to exist in him, that had attracted me. But Dudley was not my ideal—far from it. It was he himself, by no help of imagination, who had forced me into owning to myself that he was more to me than ever any ideal, any piece of impossible perfection could be; and as unaided he had won this place, so nothing on earth but his own act could dethrone him now.

Must I think less of him?—think he had lowered his old standard, fallen away from his old ideas, and was only entering into a compact by which he would receive on the one hand so much more money during his life (the most uncertain of all tenures; it may be for five years—it may be for fifty—who knows?), and that with the other hand he was flinging away the truth, honour, and self-respect without which he would be unrecognisable, and which had been as necessary to him as the air he breathed. Impossible! I would not think so, because, woman-like, I did not wish to do so; better think anything than think of him as lowered. No; Mrs. Lascelles had been his first love years before; was even lovelier than ever, and was a woman of the world whose birth, breeding, and knowledge of society would all help to make her understand quickly, and be as readily appreciated by, a man of her own circle and experiences in life. He cared for her still, could never really have ceased caring for her. His old smouldering love had been fanned once more into passion, and even if her character were weak and spiteful in my eyes, his were happily blinded, and old memories, and the same external habits and modes of life, common friends and familiar grooves in society (though as a younger son he had hollowed out a fresh one for himself) would in the fitness of things suit them for each other, and prevent any outward jar or clash in their lives.

Having settled, after some days, all which in my own mind, I seemed to be on sure ground once again. Day after day I went about with my aunt, visiting her favourite poor district and sick children; working and helping my best and learning lessons of self-abnegation which would help to make my future passive existence useful to others, and, in consequence, happier to myself.

Preparations for the wedding went on rapidly, and in March I was to return with my cousin and her husband by New York, as Gerald wished to see something of the

States, when the opportunity was so good.

Day by day I was more satisfied to leave Sophia, who seemed now so contented and happy, that I could never again have any doubts as to her future. And for myself, I was quite ready to return to Ireland; since, having seen with my own eyes my one sister's welfare, it only remained to see that of the other, and be its chronicler in these pages.—What fairer ending to this tale of myself than merging self in that gentlest and perhaps most sympathetic of life-loves, springing from one source, fed on the same joys and griefs, during growing years of shine and rain?

My own passionate theme had been played rapidly, and was ended; the rest of the music in my life would be only low and monotonous, with occasional memories of the old air mingling with its subdued harmony. Even so; what is, is best; and though not one of my old dreams of being a principal actor in the din, and stir, and bustle of this world, would ever come to pass, yet how seldom are our anticipations realised; or, if so, do they still satisfy us, who change our natures in some slight degree with every changing year? Nay, we look rather back at the hollow gilded baubles of our bygone years with faint wondering smiles that such should ever have given us that old foolish joy; so might oldened, life-wearied Roman men have looked at the golden *bullæ* of their boyhood's days—well for us if, like them, we make them votive offerings at the shrine of our God, when the turning-point in our lives too comes, and a nobler, manlier ambition fires our hearts and glorifies our lives.

CHAPTER VIII.

A WIND THAT BLOWS SOMEBODY LUCK.

"There's tempest in yon hornéd moon,
And lightning in yon cloud;
And hark! the music, mariners,
The wind is piping loud."

"WELL, this is not exactly the cheerfullest day nor the brightest city I have ever seen." And so saying, I almost slipped, as, following Gerald Forbes, and his newly-married wife, my feet touched the wet, treacherous deck of the *New Orleans*. A sharp, biting, vicious March wind blew round us, between the funnels of our steamer, through the masts and rigging of all the shipping around, and through and through our bones, it seemed, also, for the matter of that. Behind us lay New York, almost blotted out from our eyes by the waterfall of chilling rain which was streaming down around us, filling the gutters, soaking through our boots, making its way through our waterproofs, and finding a sly watercourse unto itself down the nape of Gerald's neck, while our umbrellas seemed divided between a desire to take a flight in the wind, or turn inside out upon the spot.

Despite the weather, there was a busy crowd of dripping men and wet carriages on the pier. On board, the decks were crowded with piles of luggage, and limp groups of passengers, all in their ugliest weather-proof garments, saying good-bye to friends who made frantic efforts to embrace them under their umbrellas, knocked each other's noses, and sawed hands violently up and down, just as the order to "cast off" was heard above the noise and confusion, the running up and down of sailors, loosening of ropes and escaping of steam. There was a rush on shore —a shout or two—a motion under our feet, and we were off—back on our way to Queenstown, in the *New Orleans.*

"I do believe we were the very, very last to get on deck, Gerald. What a mercy you did not make us quite late, you lazy man!" said Susan, as we stood together, three grim figures, looking as if we had just been drawn through a river.

"Some one must be last, and I believe one loses a great deal of precious time by being too early," answered her husband, with even more coolness than usual, which, as his teeth were chattering with cold, was hardly to be wondered at.

I was shivering too, all over, and just then coughed violently, as I had often done of late.

"Oh, that dreadful cough! It quite racks through one's brain. Do go down below and get dry, Queenie," exclaimed my cousin, waking up at the sound from contemplating alternately the receding shores and her husband's decidedly cold, blue-looking countenance as she leant on his arm. "I'll go too and help you."

"That you shan't," I answered, as pleasantly as a very hoarse throat and a sharp pain in my chest would allow me. "You want to see the last of your native land, I know. Perhaps I *had* better get dried; though I am so thorougly soaked now, a little more rain would hardly hurt me."

"Upon my word, I think you had," said

Gerald, turning sharply, as another fit of coughing shook me. "You are worse than ever to-day, and you have had this cold all the last fortnight we have been in the States. Take my advice, and go straight to your berth at once, and try to get rid of that chill. Susan, we have not been looking half after her;" and he eyed me anxiously as I departed.

One's berth so early in the evening seems far from an inviting idea, yet when I reached the small cabin—which, luckily, owing to the small number of passengers, was to be mine by undisputed right of possession—my limbs were so chilled and aching, and the feeling of oppression on my chest was so great, that I made only a faint show of resistance when Susan and her maid overpowered me with cordials and remedies, and forced me to lie down.

There was no use in trying to hide from myself the fact that I felt really ill; the cough which had settled upon me lately was much worse, and I seemed to have little strength left to fight against it; so I was destined to make close acquaintance with that tiny cabin, its porthole, its two berths, dismal washstand, and long sofa, for that day, and the next and the next.

"I'm coming to cheer you up a little," said Susan, with her beaming face, entering the said cabin that evening after tea, and plumping down on the sofa with her usual energy. "Oh, dear! What do you think? Gerald is taken bad already;" and she went off into a fit of laughing. "Hadn't hardly touched his tea, poor fellow, when he rose and fled with a look of the horrors."

"And you dutifully bounced after him, I suppose?" I answered, with a weary yawn.

"But it is getting rather rougher already. We must be some little way outside the harbour now, I suppose."

"He says it is not sickness—oh dear, no, not at all; but that a dreadful American beside him kept breaking his egg into a tumbler and stirring it up, which jarred upon his sensitive nerves. Memo. for me—don't have nerves at sea," she added, going off gaily to rally the invalid close by.

Some people's animal spirits reminded me irresistibly of different species of the lower creation living with and around us—chattering magpies, frisky kittens, voracious hogs grunting out their satisfaction over a full meal—or, pleasanter, gleeful, twittering little birds; but my cousin's high spirits, added to her large figure, and constant though heavy gambols, could bring nothing else to my mind than a handsome, big-eyed, and everlastingly playful cow.

"Seems he was all wrong about the egg," she remarked, coming back again after an hour or so, and once more subsiding audibly upon the sofa. "Our last conclusion is that they give one too many small dishes at the New York hotels for breakfast. I thought he ate too many fixings, and that's a solemn fact." Whereupon Mrs. Gerald Forbes gave a heavy sigh, though her eyes still looked remarkably lively.

I swallowed an execrable cough-lozenge, and answered, it is to be regretted, with hoarse, sleepy peevishness,

"Why, if people *will* eat hot, half-cooked bread for breakfast,—and surround themselves with a battery of small dishes,—and devour them all, though they are greasy and half cold——"

"Why, they must expect to feel jarred

rather in the nerves," she laughed. "But what is wrong with you, any way?"

"I think I am ill, and I am very certain I am cross," was my truthful answer; so, as it was almost time for the lights to be extinguished in our cabins, Susan pitied me, and said good night.

The third day of our voyage out still found both Gerald Forbes and myself suffering respectively from cold and sea-sickness.

"What a pity you don't try and come into the saloon—it might brighten you up a little, and some of the people are great fun," said Susan, coming to visit me after the dinner at four o'clock, or "eight bells," as we had learned to call it. "At meals, now, it is quite amusing. The Captain has me on his right hand, and is really lively, though he does look like a sanctimonious spider; and on my other side is a stern

Englishman, and beyond him again a terrible old lady from the West, in a bright green silk and magenta ribbons, who says she reckons she'll wake him up, and not let him raise a sleep, if he were the silentest, starchedest Britisher that ever was."

"And does she attack him, then?" I asked, with the languid curiosity of an invalid, to whom every scrap of outside news was a real boon.

"Just rather. 'Stranger, do tell,' she begins, as soon as she seizes her knife (the fork is of no consequence, my dear, in her style of eating)—'do tell, stranger, whar do you come from?' He said from New York—quite politely, but shortly. 'Do tell,' she starts again, 'whar from before that?' He answered her with the name of some station; she asked still further and further, till they got south, as far as New

Orleans, with her invariable 'do tell' going all the while, and nothing but just the names of the places, and a queer smile or a bow from him. 'So, stranger,' she finishes up at last, 'you come from New Orleans to New York, and you're a Britisher at that. Your name is Dudley, I guess, for I read it over your shoulder on a letter this morning.'"

"*What* name did she say?"

"She said Dudley. Don't look as if you were going to mesmerise me."

"Oh, it was only—I know that name—what is he like?" was my reply, turning my head with a nervous laugh, and sinking down again.

"Like? Well, let's see. I was really so occupied with my agreeable Captain that I hardly looked. Stay, though; he has a dark brownish beard, I think, and speaks very little. He comes from Liverpool, and is going back there again, if that is any help."

"Not the same," I answered, in my shamed revulsion of feeling. "The one I knew was in Ireland, and had no beard."

How even the sirname of a strange passenger renewed the feeling that only misery which must be fought against awaited me in Ireland! Susan, apparently finding me absent and monosyllabic, went on deck to "get a good blowing," and how glad I was to be alone! It was not a wonderful coincidence, certainly, yet it terrified by revealing with a flash to me the true misery and shame of a love which ought no longer to exist. But I was weak and ill that day, or surely I should have crushed it in my heart.

Weak, certainly, or I should hardly have broken down so utterly as I did,—burying my head, and stifling my low sobs in the pillow, till their suppression shook me painfully from head to foot. "What is the use of trying to deceive myself any longer? I have not got over it—I cannot!—I cannot! Will it never be the same fresh feeling any more?" So I moaned in my weak, nerveless wretchedness, recognising with a dumb cry of misery the vast difference between this and all former troubles. "It shall—it must. Why can my pride not help me? If he has forgotten, why should I remember? Yet all the while I knew that it never would be quite the same again—never! All hope had died for me since I had seen that other woman in his arms. Life might be borne patiently, humbly, but never again would my future path seem flooded with sunshine, winding away into distance like a golden ribbon of light. Never again should I waken up to walk my appointed day's journey along it with the old gladness and elasticity—the pure joy of *being* alive. Once before sorrow had made life a winter to me, but a fresh, bright spring had followed; now it could only be one long, dull, grey season, till the clouds darkened still lower and deeper—and, oh! how often is that time longed for—the sooner the better—by tired human souls, who would so gladly, so thankfully, lie down and be at rest!

It had been blowing ever since we left New York, but this night the wind freshened still more, and the *New Orleans* proved but a rough cradle to all her passengers, as we were bumped and tossed and shaken to and fro by our stepmother, the angry sea. But no cradle song could have brought much sleep to my eyes that night, had all nature been as peaceful as the sleepiest summer noontide, instead of wild, stormy March.

The ghosts of what dead things I had tried to bury so deep had left their graves to-night, and were all abroad, dancing a mocking, maddening saturnalia in my brain, and would not suffer themselves to be laid till what time cocks should crow in far-off lands, and these phantoms of former happy moments, bitter-sweet looks and tones and words which *would* not be forgotten, should pale like the stars under the kindly light, and the day assert its healthier influence. But now, in the murk night, I lie in my berth, and think, and think, with ever-recurring, useless regrets; for

> "The tender grace of a day that is dead,
> Will never come back to me."

All the past, and that one figure in it *dead!*—for me, at least, dead for ever. Yet all through the noises of the wind; the creaking vibration of the ship's timbers as she fought her way against the gale which blew right in her teeth, while heavy seas broke over her occasionally; the sounds of winds and waters and screws seemed to resolve themselves into a discordant, dirge-like accompaniment, to one name which kept repeating itself over and over again in rhythmical monotony, and that name was "Dudley Wyverne! Dudley Wyverne!"

When morning came, the wind had lessened a little, though the sea was still running in sweeps of cold, green rollers, but my cough felt better, and my cabin had proved so dismal an abode that I resolved to pay a visit to the saloon.

"I mean to get up, Susan," was accordingly my decided announcement.

"What! Queen? Just as the wind gets up, too. Stay quiet, you wilful girl! Why, last night we were only going two knots an hour, or even less; and even I feel rather queer to-day."

"Then I *will* get up, if only to show you how good a sailor I am," I answered, in my perversity; and so (somewhat totteringly, from the double effects of staying in bed, and the pitching of the ship) I made my first appearance in the saloon with Susan, where we were glad to find anchorage on one of the comfortable, maroon velvet sofas, and take possession of a spare chess-board.

"We don't want rocking-chairs much, do we?" observed our nearest passenger, a fragile, nervously sensitive little lady, from the Southern States, to whom I thereupon began talking (not believing, as some people do, that pleasantness to strangers is seed flung upon the waters, which will never be repaid by loaves, as in the old typical Eastern harvest-ground), and was rewarded by finding in her quite a mine of belief in mesmerism, spiritualism, and biology of every shade, which I accordingly studied with half-interest, half-amusement, as a new experience.

Soon afterwards a large lady loomed in the doorway, whom Susan's hearty sigh and low-breathed utterance of "*That woman!*" proclaimed at once to be her female aversion from the West; she, casting a glance of scorn towards us as she *collided* hither and thither with the ship's lurches, proceeded, when seated, to designate us with one finger to her neighbours, informing them that our companion was "a Creole, or a Secess, from down South somewhar; that good-looking stranger" (meaning me, who simply state the fact, and care little now whether it be true or not) "would be a Britisher, she guessed," while Susan was supposed to come from some down-trodden hole in Queen Vicky's dominions—a Blue-nose, according to the likeliest calculations.

"She hates me, for we came up from Jacksonville in the cars with her party," observed the little Southerner confidingly to me, for whom she seemed to have conceived an instantaneous liking. "She was a widow quite lately, they say; very rich, for her first husband struck oil, but he was shot once too often in the street six months ago, and then she pounced on this poor little pocket-edition of a man."

"He reminds one of the Widow's Mite," I made reply, looking at the lady's scared little husband, who seemed divided between terror of his larger half and of the tossing of our good ship.

We remained in the saloon some time longer, but every quarter of an hour it seemed to get rougher and rougher, until at last, just as our new acquaintance had excited Susan's envy, and my incredulity, by her tales of a marvellously spiritualistic housemaid in the family of a friend, who had the power of moving the heaviest wooden beds or wardrobes by one push of her hand, owing to the possession of some peculiar influence ("an invaluable gift for a person in her station of life," as I opined)—just then, I repeat, Mrs. Gerald Forbes herself—oh! shattered pride!—oh! downfall and desolation!—she, of all people in the world, was fain to retreat ignominiously to that friendly cabin whose privacy already sheltered her husband, in his lonely misery, from the unsympathising gaze of those few fellow-passengers on board who did not share his feelings and his circumstances.

"There is that Mr. Dudley, now. Look,

Queen, look," she whispered, quickly, as we were leaving the saloon.

And I looked—in my haste being knocked up against two tables by an equal number of pitchings—but only saw, for my pains, a pair of legs clad in dark-blue serge ascending on deck—a last glimpse of the owner's boots, but no more. Then, not caring to stay without my cousin, I regained my cabin-door, after some wild and apparently misguided lurches; but what a sight presented itself! All my worldly goods on board the *New Orleans* (few though they were, yet precious on that very account) were in full career over the cabin, chasing each other madly up and down, and it was only by sitting down on the floor, and making wild grasps at each object which bobbed successively within my reach, that they could at last all be safely stowed away.

The wind seemed to rise every minute. By-and-by ensued such a rattling of crockery, and shouting of sailors, who were now all rushing about in tarpaulins and long boots, that there could be no doubt about it—we were in for stormy weather; which lasted, indeed, with some violence, during most of that night; but, thanks, perhaps, to my previous wakefulness, I was able, nevertheless, to close my tired eyes, and sleep the sound sleep of utter weariness.

"Let us go up on deck, and see the waves, Susan," I valiantly proposed, about eleven o'clock A.M. of the next day—half an hour before which time we first had courage to leave our berths. "It will be splendid. They must still be running mountains high."

"But, oh! Queenie—Gerald told me to take such care of you."

"But, oh! Susan, the view! And Mr.

Gerald is safe in his berth," I mimicked, basely inciting her to covert rebellion, while her lord and master was but feebly maintaining existence upon champagne, and an occasional hard biscuit nibbled during the day.

Up on deck we accordingly ventured, holding tight by the nearest railing, and gazing with half-exultation, half-timidity, as the splendid sight of those magnificent Atlantic rollers met our eyes, and now and then a shower of salt spray would leap up and come over us, wetting our waterproofs. The wind had abated a good deal, but it was still blowing from the north-east, cresting Neptune's horses with white manes, while occasional gleams of March sun fitfully lighted up broad bands of the green heaving mountains and valleys of water which alternately towered or sank around us.

"Hold tight, Susan. Doesn't this remind you of our nursery days? Now we go up, up, up; and now we go down, down, down," I gasped, as the stern of the ship seemed to sink beneath us, one hardly knew where, and the vessel itself was apparently ambitious of standing upright on one end; another few moments, and we had climbed a looming mountain before us, and poising on its crest, surveyed proudly for a second the world of waters tossing, heaving, and tumbling far around us, only to glide away swiftly once more down the side of the glassy, yawning chasm below.

We were the only ladies, almost the only passengers, to be seen on deck; so the Captain, espying us, came to speak to Mrs. Forbes, who was a general favourite, owing to her good looks and liveliness.

"You will get a thorough wetting, ladies,"

he observed, after complimenting us on our courage. "By the way, Mrs. Forbes, you wanted to have a peep into our smoking-room. There is no one there now, I fancy, if you like to come."

But though curiosity made us both feel tempted to invade for once the comfortable-looking little house on deck, sacred to the rites of the goddess veiled in smoke, prudence overcame valour, and the friendly Captain was despatched as a spy, to report, "if there was anyone in it?"

"There is only our English friend who sits beside you at dinner and another also, a young officer. You know them both, Mrs. Forbes, and they are most anxious to do the honours."

As the door opened I caught sight of a shining waterproof coat, and felt an irresistible temptation to make the acquaintance of this unknown individual whose sirname was the same as that Christian one which so lately I had uttered in fond secresy to myself as the sweetest name to me on earth. I had heard no particulars about Dudley Wyverne's marriage with Mrs. Lascelles as yet, since Nellie's last letters had been full of other subjects, and Aunt Emily I had shrunk from asking; while her few letters would, if properly edited, have made a good homily on the sins and shortcomings of mankind or girlhood, or, indeed, most of the human race in general, always excepting herself.

Just then I heard a voice——

"*Merciful heavens!*"

A gust of wind flapped my waterproof cape round my head, while a sudden shower of spray half-blinded me, as I caught by the door for support; but that voice would still have reached my ears had all the four winds at once been bellowing round us, and the fountains of the deep been broken up,—(as they seemed to be, so blinded and deafened was I with surging, booming waves pulsating through my head and brain from the sudden shock)—and the voice said, politely—too courteously to be genuinely glad,

"Pray come in, Mrs. Forbes. You are not one of those ladies to whom one would offer a cigarette; but that makes it all the more the greatest honour which has yet been paid us—*by—Jove!*"

No more, as my face appeared in the doorway, when "Goodness gracious!" burst from Susan. "Have a care there." "Mind the ladies," from the others; for a sudden pitch forward of the ship had precipitated us all pell-mell into the furthest end of the little cabin.

"You are not hurt?—tell me you are not hurt—Miss Demeric," and *Dudley!*—

Dudley himself only added the latter expression in deference to the laws of formality, as he saw that the fervour of his anxiety and the warmth of his grasp raised an amused, wondering smile on the faces of the rest. "I had not the very faintest idea!—if I had only but known you were on board——"

"I am coming back from Canada with Mrs. Forbes; Mr. Gerald Forbes married my cousin, the Canadian Miss Demeric, don't you know?" and as I strove to explain matters with would-be composure, my voice was as unsteady as his own.

"This is a new pleasure, Mrs. Forbes. I never guessed you were dear old Gerald's wife. He and I were always such friends."

In the surprise of these explanations, we all looked shaken out of our birthright of frigidity, and prepared for any fresh link in this chain of acquaintanceship. Then the others—was it by accident or design?—fell to examining studiously the damages of a meerschaum pipe, which its owner, one of our English passengers, had just rescued in pieces from under somebody's feet; while Dudley—his face flushing a little, with an eager, excited look in his eyes, a little changed by his beard, perhaps, and in a rough pea-jacket, but still with the same handsome, dear old face which had come so often to me with loving, kindly eyes in my dreams—Dudley said, as we stood somewhat apart,

"*How* glad I am to see you! It is like a dream, only that in my wildest dreams I never imagined such a joy as this. To think that you were on board, within a few feet of me, and never to guess it—not to *feel* you were there!"

And I answered nothing as yet, only looked back at him blankly at first, then with a curious expression of defiance; for now—now he must never guess how my pulses were throbbing and my heart beating thick and fast at every look of delight, each warmly-whispered word of gladness. And—what did he mean by it?

"I am on my way home from New Orleans," he continued, never heeding, in his eagerness, that I did not answer him—"launched again, you see, in my old line of business. I got the offer, and went out there very shortly after you left Ireland."

"After—I—left—Ireland?"

The words fell slowly one by one in my faltering, puzzled want of comprehension.

"Are you—are you alone, then?"

"Of course I am. What else should I be?"

"They wrote to me—or rather, that is, I fancied, you would have been married by now."

"Married! *No!*—nor going to be—that is to say . . . Well, I declare the inventions of some people beat everything—everything under heaven. As if any one but you could ever be—"

And what might not have reached other ears than my happy, tingling ones, will never now be known, for either Susan disliked the atmosphere of fragrant tobacco fumes, or else she had no more interested observations to make on that most blessed meerschaum, that pipe of peace and happiness to me; or else she thought it time to beat a graceful retreat from the foreign domain we had entered—anyhow, she called me away; but I had heard all I wanted.

CHAPTER IX.

AND ALL WENT MERRY AS A MARRIAGE BELL.

"We parted: sweetly gleamed the stars,
And sweet the vapour-braided blue,
Low breezes fann'd the belfry bars,
As homeward by the church I drew.
The very graves appeared to smile,
So fresh they rose in shadow'd swells.
'Dark porch,' I said, 'and silent aisle,
There comes a sound of marriage bells.'"

TWO grave young people, looking in each other's eyes, with that expression of sadness which even the happiest of the living wear when speaking tenderly and reverently of even those dead most blessed.

"So he told me himself to thank you," softly says the one. "I wonder" (reflectively)—"I wonder *could* you possibly ever do anything that was not generous or kind."

"Couldn't I, my Queen? Just wait till you know me a little better; and as to generosity, it cost me a terrible struggle to help poor Graham, as I fancied, to get you. I don't believe if it was to come over again that I could do it; and now that you *do* like me, I give you fair warning I'll give you up to no one on the face of this earth."

"And you are *quite* sure you did not like Mrs. Lascelles, then—just a little, don't you know?"

"Don't you know?" he mimics, laughing outright in his fondness. "I do know, and am *quite* sure, that this is one of the most foolish little ladies in the world—always jumping to the worst conclusions, and then making herself needlessly unhappy. I went down to Maghrenagh about that wretched business, and she asked me in to lunch. I was as much surprised and annoyed as you were, I give you my word."

"Who said I was surprised or unhappy either, you vain man?" (Oh! Queenie Demeric, what a terribly black fib that sentence involved!) "But—but why did you write that letter?"

"It was necessary, darling, don't you see? I could not have been happy in my own mind had I not left you free; though I *hoped*——"

"Never mind your hopes now, sir. I only wonder"—(with the touch of malice which still remained as a trace of the old vindictiveness)—"I only wonder you were hard-hearted enough to refuse her offer."

If such a thing were possible, or at least

visible, one would almost say that that browned, tanned, hardened old Dudley blushed; then, finding himself thus made uncomfortable at the remembrance of the embarrassment of that former situation, he basely bethought himself of a mode of action by which I was in my turn put out of countenance, and prevented, for the moment at least, from making any more such disagreeable speeches.

"We can afford to forgive Mrs. Lascelles now, can't we, darling? Let us leave her alone, eh? Or rather," with a happy laugh, "let us leave her to her husband, Captain Heavyman. How was it you missed seeing her marriage in the *Times?*"

So said the magnanimous victor in the late tactics, while the humble, vanquished one answered nothing, because, being oppressed by a sense of their perilous situation, she hardly knew what to say! Flight from the saloon, of which they were the solitary occupants, offering itself as the most prudent course; though there is the lowering probability that the superior force of Mr. Dudley Wyverne might have interposed to prevent it. And even if such were not the case, and escape perfectly feasible, it is just doubtful, with that fine, hair's-breadth nicety of doubt which keeps both scales trembling all but evenly on the balance, whether Miss Queenie Demeric would have seen it in the light of such a very particularly desirable advantage.

It was that exact time of the morning chosen by all the ship's passengers to walk up and down the deck, leaving the saloon a desert, and as it was also a remarkably fine, sunny day, nothing could be more natural, under the circumstances, than that

I should have betaken myself to the most secluded corner of the said saloon—to read; or that Dudley should also, about the same time, have found his way thither—to fetch a book, of course; or that, struck with innocent surprise at the unexpected coincidence, we should have seated ourselves on the same sofa, to read and compare notes on our separate studies, also very much as a matter of course. And what those notes were, or how the reading progressed, cannot possibly signify to the impertinent curiosity of the outside public.

"But you know, Queenie, dearest, that I am quite a poor man again." As he spoke the ghost of a shadow flitted across Dudley's handsome face, which yet looked absurdly, supremely happy, while he made this announcement.

"I know," with a little nod, as if, the

matter being fully understood, there was no need to discuss it further.

"But you don't know, my pet," stretching round his head to look more fully in my face. "You don't know how hard it is on a man not to be able to give his wife all the luxuries he would like. Don't you remember my telling you that you ought always to drive in a barouche, and be dressed in——"

"*Mr. Wyverne!*" in blazing indignation, with my head very much upright.

"Well, there, there; then we'll say no more on that subject. Only—suppose the climate of New Orleans should not agree with you?"

"It *shall* agree with me!"

Dudley looked delighted; but at once cast about in his own mind for a fresh opportunity of exercising that most delicious occupation of teasing, of which the results generally give additional piquancy to what might be otherwise happiness almost too *same* in its perfection. Or is the boy so much father to the man that his bliss is not complete in later years without a trace of the old enjoyment, though in a garb far more pleasurable to the female mind?

"But supposing your guardians make no end of objections!—never let me see you till you come of age!—I believe I shall have to run off with—— Queenie, dearest, don't look like that! Don't you know I was only talking nonsense?"

For when highly-strung nerves are so over-wrought as mine by repeated wretchedness, strange scenes and faces, and sudden, overwhelming happiness, all succeeding each other, and seeming now to have been crowded into the past two hours, so vividly have they rushed back, one is but a musical instrument, whose every string answers when swept by the one master-hand, and happiness seems to some so much more unreal than misery, that just now I quivered with anticipations of pain responsive to his words. Surely it was all a dream, which would fade and dissolve as so many before; and so thinking, I looked blankly down the saloon before us. Its tables and sofas, and the unfamiliar air and heaving motion would perhaps all come back to memory in some living, sad future; it could not be *true*, that other future, in the far sunny south, which a voice beside me whispered of so tenderly, so late. Had not quick pain always followed my short-lived pleasures? No, this was but a momentary illusion of ours, our delirious bliss a dream, and the happily fateful *New Orleans* but "a painted ship upon a painted ocean!"

A hand took both mine in its large, warm grasp, and quieted by its feeling of strength my vibrating nerves—strength to overcome for me what I felt too weak and powerless to struggle against by myself; and even without looking round, I felt the presence beside me, was aware of the gaze which brought back the old warmth and light again, and listened dreamily to the half tender, half joking tones, which changed the discords back at once into the old harmony.

Just then a high-pitched nasal voice outside makes me give a guilty start, and the voice says unmelodiously,

"Wal, I guess, stranger, you *are* about right. It *was* cold at breakfast, and not the length of a flea-jump would that nasty French frog beside me stir, though I says to him, 'Mister or Mossoo,' says I, '*fummle a port*, or we'll all be blowed away!'"

"Oh, Dudley!—that odious Yankee woman! *Please* let me go on deck."

"By-and-by; don't be so excitable. You know you are reading," answered that gentleman, with exasperating placidity. "What trouble I foresee in quieting down your impulsiveness!" And he smiled fondly, with his head rather on one side, and a strange light in his eyes—apparently more than willing to prolong the situation for an interminable length of time.

"But, Dudley—*dear* Dudley——"

So, after a time, I was allowed to have my own way *this once*, and to go on deck to rejoin the Forbes'.

"But do just tell me, Dudley: am I—am I all right?" was my anxious query before departure, glancing in the mirror, despite his laughing observations on my vanity; for somehow or another my face *felt* scarified, and I could not rid myself of the impression that it *looked* it.

"You look quite guilty," answered that most tiresome individual. "What a tell-tale face you have, to be sure! Anyone will see by it in a moment that you have been a very naughty girl."

Upon receiving which comforting assurance, I sailed out of the saloon with my head very high in the air, trying hard not to smile, but to meet his teasing with the most stately dignity.

And on deck we came upon Gerald Forbes and his bonnie wife, the former of whom observed reflectively that a sea voyage was a wonderful cure for some people's coughs. "For instance, Miss Demeric here has quite got back her colour again." Furthermore remarking to me aside, without *àpropos*, that his sister Bella was always delighted to be bridesmaid to anyone, as her stock of lockets was low; while Susan adds in her turn—to the surrounding air—that the *New Orleans* certainly *was* a wonderful ship, in more ways than one. "And did Mr. Wyverne think (as a matter of curiosity) that the climate of South America or New Orleans itself, for example, would be equally beneficial to people who had coughs or colds, or that sort of thing?"

. . . .

What remains yet to tell? The turning-point of my life has come; the tale told, the theme played out; but yet one's fingers still stray lovingly among the notes, striking some faint final chords, as one who yet lingers with a pleasant regret over the memory of that past sweet time which has been to each of us—that time "when all the world was young."

In due course of time our good ship arrived at Queenstown, though not without having endured previously some more buffeting from winds and waves, which made the funnels, and even the very smoke-stacks, white from the salt sea-spray. Then, though his business obliged Dudley to go on to Liverpool, the rest of us travelled up happily towards the Black North, where the inmates of Ballymore were aroused out of their usual practical cut-and-dried ways into a warm welcome; while a still warmer one awaited me at Craigowrie, whose pretty mistress now assumed the airs of the most fashionable of lively little matrons imaginable, and whose delight was unbounded when my great secret was slowly and mysteriously confided to her most sympathising ears. "Though what Uncle Alick will say to it, I don't know," is the ending of my tale.

To which terrible suggestion it is to be feared that Nell answered airily, in the fearlessness of her emancipation, that she supposed I should let Uncle Alick say just what he pleased.

"Then you know," she went on confidentially, "*his* elder brother is an invalid, and says he never will marry, so you might be Lady Wyverne, and take precedence of me some of these days."

Whereat I shook my head decidedly, opining that I was quite content to be the wife of a younger son, without regard to any such dim uncertainties; yet, very possibly, when we had spent two winters in New Orleans, they might find Dudley coming back quite a well-to-do, though perhaps not a rich man.

"Then, as Uncle and Aunt are tired of Ballymore, you can take it off Sophia's hands, and we shall both be living close to each other, and driving over every other day," cried Nellie, boldly sketching out the future. "And indeed, my dear old Queen, I can't wish you more than to be just as happy as I am. Not that Bob there is not the plague of my life," she added hastily, lest that gentleman (whom she thought had rather a turn that way), should be led for one moment to believe himself particularly precious. "I am certain that you, for instance, never could put up with him; and perhaps I should find your Mr. Dudley quite as tiresome."

Whereat the much-enduring beauty gave a faint, elegant grunt from his easy-chair, as he indulged in the sacred weed (even Bob's grunts have a sort of lazy grace about them), and he aroused himself to remark, with his legs easily crossed, and his eyes following a cloud of smoke curling towards the ceiling—for we were in the billiard-room—that marriage has taught him we have all much to put up with, but for his part he is resigned. Dear old Dudley being the very best fellow he knows, will probably be the same; and "so long as you're happy, what's the odds?"

Our surmises as to Uncle Alick's probable behaviour proved, however, incorrect; for when the news reached him (I meanwhile being safely ensconced in Craigowrie), it was Aunt Emily who, with her usual vehemence, at once declared that the whole thing was absurd, ridiculous, and perfectly preposterous!

"Marry Mr. Wyverne *now! I never heard of such a thing!* And, besides, he is a man I never could feel at ease with."

Here Bob, who, with Mr. Burke, made up the fateful trio, hazarding the consoling remark that it was not Mrs. Burke whom Dudley wished to spend his life with, was most properly withered by a lightning glance.

"But," continued the lady, giving vent to her outraged feelings, "I never expected anything better of Queenie—never! Only I can tell her, if she expects me to say yes, she is uncommonly mistaken. I couldn't *think* of such a thing."

"Ye . . . couldn't?" asked Mr. Burke, slowly, with an ominous calm, and an equally ominous Irish accent. Mrs. Burke looked at him, and quailed a little; then, to recover her courage, she rose up a little from her chair, re-seating herself with an emphatic thud. She ought to have known better; but she did it.

"No, Alick, I won't allow it—not for a moment!"

"Not—for—a—moment?" and Mr. Burke

eyed her meditatively for three seconds—the fourth, and he brought down his fist with a bang.

"Then, by George! I WILL!"

Without one word Aunt Emily rose, and swept in gaunt majesty from the apartment, her spouse satirically nodding an accompaniment to her retiring steps, then, turning about, winked to Kingston confidentially, and remarked, with grim humour,

"Believe me, Robert, the only time to give a woman her own way is *when you can't help* it! And if I did not give Queenie hers with a good grace now, maybe very soon she might *take it.*"

"And," said Bob, afterwards, as he told the story, "to see the old fellow's red face and knowing look was really splendid. By Jove it was!"

Whereupon we all laughed a little, and

agreed that when Miss Nora grew up she would yet give her guardian some trouble as to his theories, for no small young lady in short dresses was ever more dictatorial, or, by bestowing her mighty favours alternately between uncle and aunt, managed so completely to have her own way.

Poor Aunt Emily's bark proved, however, worse than her bite; she bowed to fate; and though for some days we received dark hints of threatening heart-disease, paralysis, or numerous nervous maladies, which were all being hurried upon her by my alleged ingratitude, still she gradually relented, perceiving that Dudley's poverty offered a grand field for constant lectures on economy, and interference in domestic arrangements, which, unfortunately, 'Robert Kingston was so queer-tempered, he would not allow, never giving her the chance of saying even a single word to that little goose of a Nellie;' and finally she grew quite cheerful over the preparations, remarking, however, to the dowager Mrs. Kingston, who sighed and swayed her black bonnet from side to side ominously,

"At all events the young couple will not have long to make fools of themselves, since you know, Euphrasia, it is now certain that about the 7th of September next we may expect the End of All Things; and, indeed," (meditatively), "I wrote to Sophia that, under the circumstanccs, I had not thought it worth while to plant any more Wellingtonias!"

Then, in the spring having gone over to London with Nellie, whom should we come upon one morning in the Row but the late Mrs. Lascelles, now Mrs. Heavyman. Her husband, my old aversion, had grown stouter, coarser, and more addicted to a club-life than ever; and informed us boisterously that they had spent their honeymoon at Nice, or rather at the gambling-table of Monte Carlo. And she—heaven help her!—had already begun again to shrug her shoulders faintly, and look round with those appealing blue eyes, mutely asking sympathy from other men, as she had looked while Joe Lascelles—poor, easy-tempered soul—was alive, and made him a different man from what he might have been. Almost as pretty as ever; though the beautiful colour is hardly natural, the smiles more forced, and that shading under the eye-lashes has been freshly put on. So she will smile on, and lay her pretty traps year by year, till the face grows more raddled and powdered and wrinkled, and no one cares any longer to hear her pitiful tale of domestic tyranny.

Heaven help such women, then, say I!

How the old poison still lurked in those honeyed words as she congratulated me, and hoped I might "prove able to keep Mr. Wyverne in order. He was always a sad flirt—sad; but perhaps you are not a jealous person. Ha! ha!"

Ah! well. She goes her way in life, and I go mine. Let us think no more of her, or try to think kindly with compassion.

And Lady Highlyffe, stately and sweet-smiling as ever, kissed me cordially, like the dearest old woman in the world that she was; and the Forbes were all brimming over with smiles, while Bella affirmed "she knew it all along, of course. Oh! there was no deceiving her!"

So the spring-time came and went slowly, like a happy dream, sliding softly into summer; the sunshine grew warm and warmer day by day, and soft winds were blowing over the greening, blossoming land, while the happy days grew longer and longer, till at last the dusk of the mysterious twilight only seemed to darken for a little, and then change and whiten slowly into the dawn and brightness of the glorious, gladdening summer mornings. And so on and on, while the skies grow bluer and deeper, the green stronger, the flowers more glowing and gorgeous; and the birds cease their piping and carolling, to rest and bask themselves, like all Nature, in the full, exhausting heat of the noontide of the year.

This was in the outer world around. But also in the narrower inner world, my life and thoughts partook of the changes in the life outside—shy, budding hopes of unlooked-for happiness expanding day by day in the sunshine of love; faint fears which still lingered like the last sheltered snow-flakes in sunny spring, melting away under those warming beams; and my being, too, like the great heart of the world without, basking itself gladly in that flooding light and warmth of love and joy and happiness.

Then came a day in August, when the happy time we had been looking forward to, as day by day it grew nearer and more real, has come at last; and I looked round at all the dear old spots, and recalled the childish associations with a smile and a sigh, for after to-morrow as Queenie Demeric I should see them no more.

How unchanged it all was!—one almost wondered. There was the sea, with its waves sparkling as of old in that dip between the wooded hills; the Long Meadow, with the young colts whinnying or staring, or taking a canter in the far corner in their happy, unbridled freedom; the old fish-pond and garden tower; the dark green of the shrubberies, while stretching down between these to the water lay the close-shaven, grassy garden, with its gaudy beds of yellow and scarlet geraniums and calceolarias dotted about between the shrubs—lower down again the straight elms and bending beeches. And I looked at it all, for many a day I should want to call the scene to mind when far away in our southern home. Then, since the dead are so closely blended with the living that we cannot, even if we would, forget those silver cords, which, though severed, are still interwoven with the threads of our past, but still living, ever-weaving lives, I turned away once more in that direction where our feet often stray—to the old church nestling itself into the shelter of the fir-wood. The sun encircled the tops of the old silver fir and spruce-trees with a golden halo, slanting warm beams across that quiet, grassy plot of ground lying there undisturbed among the other fields around, which are ploughed and tilled, sowed and reaped, year after year. God's Acre receives its seed, indeed, but the harvest must wait for many a day. And I thought of a grave far away, under Canadian daisies, with tender regret for that first beautiful dream, which, wisely and well, it may be, was so soon dispelled ; since never, perhaps, but for my sorrows, should I have wakened from my day-dreams, or looked before the morrow, or known what it was to suffer and rise braver, patient, and more pitiful for others by that suffering.

Before me the pine-branches drooped lovingly over a sheltered corner of the wall, to touch a small white tablet near larger marble ones, and all around it roses were blowing thickly in full-blossomed beauty, nestling in great, pale, yellow clusters, or strewing crimson leaves down on the carved stonework below, and, on the short, carefully-tended grass. Already on my way through life I had left these graves sorrowfully far behind on the wayside, but the crosses at their heads where as mile-stones, which, looking back, I would mark, and then resume again my path onwards—towards the goal.

Ah! where do our dead meanwhile rest in hope? How far is that Paradise, that Hades, that place of departed souls? Do the dreary wastes of the moon or Saturn hold any, while the more blessed abide in pleasanter planets, or behind the royal encircling light of the most glorious sun? Why speculate? Ah, David! Harvey! you are wiser now than I: but the silence of our dead ones is never broken, the gates never ajar. . . . Faith can picture what lies still farther beyond, and dream of the spotless beauty of that Holy City, whose jewelled and shining bulwarks seem to rise before the prophetic gaze of earnest, visionary eyes; but of that which lies between, what seer has seen, what tongue has told? . . .

But a step sounds on the gravel, and a hand presses lovingly on my shoulder; and then we two!—we two together take our last look as separate human beings at the quiet resting-place of those who sleep through sunlight and moonlight, to toil and labour no more, for their night of rest has come; but we who remain have yet something to do, for there is a great Work, of which God grant each and all of us to weave our appointed portion with the threads of our lives—weave it, it may be, in sorrow and sighing, soiled with our life's blood, and stained with our tears—yet, when finished, to be cleansed pure and spotless, and freed from all stains, white as no fuller on earth can whiten it.

* * * * * *

And the morrow rises fair, and bright, and glad.

> "'Dark porch,' I said, 'and silent aisle,
> There comes a sound of marriage bells.'"

THE END.

LONDON: PRINTED BY MACDONALD AND TUGWELL, BLENHEIM HOUSE.

MESSRS. HURST AND BLACKETT'S

LIST OF NEW WORKS.

VOLS. III. & IV. OF THE HISTORY OF TWO QUEENS: CATHARINE OF ARAGON and ANNE BOLEYN.

By W. HEPWORTH DIXON. *Second Edition.* Demy 8vo. Price 30s. Completing the Work.

"These concluding volumes of Mr. Dixon's 'History of two Queens' will be perused with keen interest by thousands of readers. Whilst no less valuable to the student, they will be far more enthralling to the general reader than the earlier half of the history. Every page of what may be termed Anne Boleyn's story affords a happy illustration of the author's vivid and picturesque style. The work should be found in every library."—*Post.*

"Mr. Dixon has pre-eminently the art of interesting his readers. He has produced a narrative of considerable value, conceived in a spirit of fairness, and written with power and picturesque effect."—*Daily News.*

"Mr. Dixon has completed in these volumes the two stories which he has narrated with so much grace and vigour. Better still, he has cast the light of truth upon incidents that have not been seen under that light before. Full of romantic and dramatic sentiment as the story of Catharine is, we think that the more absorbing interest is concentrated in the story of Anne Boleyn. Never has it been told so fully, so fairly, or so attractively."—*Notes and Queries.*

"This work throughout bears evidence of great research; and in the hands of a writer of Mr. Dixon's talents, a book on such a subject of course could not fail to be interesting. He has availed himself of all the newest lights brought out by the publications of the Master of the Rolls."—*Athenæum.*

"Mr. Dixon's book is written in a most charming style. Moreover, it is written as all history should be written; the precision of the annalist being combined with the connexion and ease of the simple narrator."—*Examiner.*

"Mr. Dixon's work is a most effective sketch, framed with considerable dramatic skill, of the leading incidents and secret springs of one of the most eventful episodes in English history."—*The Graphic.*

LIFE OF THE RT. HON. SPENCER PERCEVAL;

Including His Correspondence. By His Grandson, SPENCER WALPOLE. 2 vols. 8vo, with Portrait. 30s.

This work contains Letters from the King, the Prince Regent, the Dukes of Cumberland, Wellington, Portland, Richmond; Lords Liverpool, Grenville, Grey, Loughborough, Spencer, Wellesley, Lonsdale, Castlereagh; Mr. Pitt, Mr. Addington, Mr. Canning, and other distinguished men.

"Mr. Walpole's work reflects credit not only on his industry in compiling an important biography from authentic material, but also on his eloquence, power of interpreting political change, and general literary address. The biography will take rank in our literature, both as a faithful reflection of the statesman and his period, as also for its philosophic, logical, and dramatic completeness."—*Morning Post.*

"In Mr. Perceval's biography his grandson has undoubtedly made a valuable addition to our Parliamentary history. The book is full of interest."—*Daily News.*

'We thank Mr. Walpole for a very valuable and interesting biography, and for doing justice to the memory of one who has too long been without it."—*Standard.*

"A very useful, a very honest, and a very interesting political biography."—*Pall Mall Gazette.*

"This book shows creditable industry and a moderate impartial tone. It will have a favourable effect for Perceval's reputation, bringing out as it does in strong relief his Parliamentary abilities and exemplary character."—*Athenæum.*

"As a contribution to political and Parliamentary history Mr. Spencer Walpole's work possesses considerable value."—*Saturday Review.*

"We have been extremely interested in Mr. Walpole's book. He has added no little to our knowledge of the character of, and the springs of action in, the times of which he writes. As a Life of Perceval, by his grandson, the work is as valuable as it could be expected to be. As a contribution to history, we are justified in according to it no inconsiderable praise."—*Examiner*

MESSRS. HURST AND BLACKETT'S NEW WORKS—*Continued.*

HISTORY OF TWO QUEENS: CATHARINE OF ARAGON and ANNE BOLEYN.

By W. Hepworth Dixon. *Second Edition.* Vols. 1 & 2. Demy 8vo. 30s. Vols. 3 & 4, completing the Work, are also now ready.

"In two handsome volumes Mr. Dixon here gives us the first instalment of a new historical work on a most attractive subject. The book is in many respects a favourable specimen of Mr. Dixon's powers. It is the most painstaking and elaborate that he has yet written. . . . On the whole, we may say that the book is one which will sustain the reputation of its author as a writer of great power and versatility, that it gives a new aspect to many an old subject, and presents in a very striking light some of the most recent discoveries in English history."—*Athenæum.*

"In these volumes the author exhibits in a signal manner his special powers and finest endowments. It is obvious that the historian has been at especial pains to justify his reputation, to strengthen his hold upon the learned, and also to extend his sway over the many who prize an attractive style and interesting narrative more highly than laborious research and philosophic insight."—*Morning Post.*

"The thanks of all students of English history are due to Mr. Hepworth Dixon for his clever and original work, 'History of two Queens.' The book is a valuable contribution to English history. The author has consulted a number of original sources of information—in particular the archives at Simancas, Alcala, and Venice. Mr. Dixon is a skilful writer. His style, singularly vivid, graphic, and dramatic—is alive with human and artistic interest. Some of the incidental descriptions reach a very high level of picturesque power."—*Daily News.*

"Mr. Hepworth Dixon, in his new work, has chosen a theme at once intrinsically interesting and admirably fit for illustration by his practised and brilliant pen. The lives of Catharine of Aragon and Anne Boleyn give ample scope to a writer so clear and vivid in his descriptions, so lifelike in his portraiture, so decided in his judgment, and whose sparkling vivacity of style can be shaded off, when necessary, by such delicate touches of tenderness and pathos. For pleasant reading and very effective writing we can warmly commend Mr. Dixon's volumes." *Daily Telegraph.*

"Two fascinating volumes. It is a work of careful criticism and conscientious investigation."—*Standard.*

WORDS OF HOPE AND COMFORT TO THOSE IN SORROW.

Dedicated by Permission to The Queen. *Second Edition.* 1 vol. small 4to, 5s. bound.

"These letters, the work of a pure and devout spirit, deserve to find many readers. They are greatly superior to the average of what is called religious literature."—*Athenæum.*

"The writer of the tenderly-conceived letters in this volume was Mrs. Julius Hare, a sister of Mr. Maurice. They are instinct with the devout submissiveness and fine sympathy which we associate with the name of Maurice; but in her there is added a winningness of tact, and sometimes, too, a directness of language, which we hardly find even in the brother. The letters were privately printed and circulated, and were found to be the source of much comfort, which they cannot fail to afford now to a wide circle. A sweetly-conceived memorial poem, bearing the well-known initials, 'E. H. P.', gives a very faithful outline of the life."—*British Quarterly Review.*

"This touching and most comforting work is dedicated to The Queen, who took a gracious interest in its first appearance, when printed for private circulation, and found comfort in its pages, and has now commanded its publication, that the world in general may profit by it. A more practical and heart-stirring appeal to the afflicted we have never examined."—*Standard.*

"These letters are exceptionally graceful and touching, and may be read with profit."—*Graphic.*

MESSRS. HURST AND BLACKETT'S NEW WORKS—*Continued.*

REMINISCENCES OF A SOLDIER. By Col. W. K. Stuart, C.B. 2 vols. crown 8vo. 21s.

"There is scarcely a page of these reminiscences but is full of entertaining matter. Colonel Stuart has told the tale of his life in a fashion that cannot fail to be appreciated by every class of reader. The book is one of the best collections of military stories we have ever seen."—*Athenæum.*

"In the course of his long service in the 86th, or Royal County Down, Colonel Stuart has visited almost every part of the widely-extended British empire, has experienced the various stirring vicissitudes of military life both in war and in peace, has had his share of adventures both perilous and amusing, and has been on intimate terms with many original 'characters,' so that his book is filled with anecdotes which inevitably excite the amusement and delight of the reader. The military man will find in these volumes a good deal that, in a professional point of view, is not only interesting but instructive."—*United Service Magazine.*

"This work will be a welcome addition to every military library. The personal anecdotes are fresh, truthful, and most amusing, and the reflections of the writer show alike the shrewd sensible man of the world and the brave practical soldier."—*United Service Gazette.*

"We have here a complete record of a varied and distinguished career passed in the famous Royal County Down Regiment. The work is written in a racy, buoyant style, and possesses an interest that never flags for an instant. Almost every page reminds us of Lever or Maxwell."—*Irish Times.*

SPAIN AND THE SPANIARDS. By Azamat Batuk. 2 vols. crown 8vo. 21s.

"Here is at last a book on Spain of the kind we have been asking for. Azamat Batuk fills his pages with his personal experiences among the armed factions who are contesting the government of the country, and describes the men who have made themselves conspicuous. Altogether, his gallery of contemporary portraits is alone sufficient to recommend his book."—*Saturday Review.*

"By the aid of this really entertaining book, the present state of the Northern Provinces of Spain may be easily divined, and the *Cosas de Espana* of the moment be brought before the mind's eye......It would be too much to say that this is the most interesting book upon Spain and the Spaniards that has appeared of late years, but many may think so after reading it."—*Athenæum.*

"A highly interesting and amusing book. In this work Azamat Batuk has made himself more enjoyable and readable than ever."—*Examiner.*

"Two clever and readable volumes. Any person who wants to know something about Spanish parties and their prospects, about the probabilities of the present civil war, or about the real inner life of the Spanish people, will do well to consult Azamat Batuk. He is generally instructive, and always entertaining."—*Scotsman.*

THROUGH RUSSIA: From St. Petersburg to Astrakhan and the Crimea. By Mrs. Guthrie. 2 vols. crown 8vo, with Illustrations. 21s.

"Mrs. Guthrie is a lively, observant, well-informed, and agreeable travelling companion. The book is interesting throughout."—*Pall Mall Gazette.*

"No book of travel within our knowledge is pleasanter to read than 'Through Russia.' It is fresh, bright, and comprehensive. Mrs. Guthrie gives us admirable descriptions of St. Petersburg, Moscow, and Astrakhan, and the voyages on the Volga and the Don are full of incident, character, and observation."—*Spectator.*

"A pleasant book to read. It contains a fair, and often very picturesque description of a part of Russia by no means familiar to tourists."—*Saturday Review.*

"A brightly-written account of a tour by St. Petersburg and Moscow, and so down the Volga and Don to the Crimea."—*Athenæum.*

"The story of Mrs. Guthrie's ramble through Russsia is at once attractive in itself, and likely to be of decided use to future travellers."—*Graphic.*

MESSRS. HURST AND BLACKETT'S NEW WORKS—*Continued.*

RECOLLECTIONS OF SOCIETY IN FRANCE AND ENGLAND. By LADY CLEMENTINA DAVIES. *Second Edition.* 2 vols. 21s.

Among numerous other distinguished persons referred to in this work are:—Louis XVI, Marie Antoinette, Louis XVIII, the Duchesse D'Angouleme, Napoleon I, the Empress Josephine, Queen Hortense, Charles X, Louis Philippe, the Duke and Duchess de Berry, the Count de Chambord, the Emperor Alexander, King Frederic William, Prince Talleyrand, Prince Esterhazy, Blucher, Ney, Soult, Fouché, the Polignacs, Talma, Napoleon III, the Empress Eugenie, the Duc de Morny, Count d'Orsay, Victor Hugo, George IV, Queen Caroline, Prince Leopold, the Princess Charlotte, the Duke of York, the Duke of Wellington, Lord Byron, Sir Walter Scott, Sir H. Davy, Tom Moore. Mr. Barham, Mrs. Siddons, the Kembles, Mrs. Jordan, Miss Stephens, Mlle. Mars, Madame Catalani, Mlle. Rachel, the Countess Guiccioli, Lady Cork, Lady Blessington, &c.

"On proceeding to a conscientious examination of the contents, we found the familiar and commonplace matter lightened and relieved by many lively touches of description, many traits of character, many illustrative incidents, which may prove helps to history, and might have been irretrievably lost had they not been marked and recorded as they occurred. Lady Clementina Davies's opportunities were excellent, and the very traditions of her family are fraught with interest. Some of her local and personal impressions are as graphic and distinct as if they had been —so to speak—photographed on her memory."—*The Times.*

"Two charming volumes, full of the most interesting and entertaining matter, and written in plain, elegant English. Lady Clementina Davies has seen much, heard much, and remembered well. Her unique and brilliant recollections have the interest of a romance, wherein no character is fictitious, no incident untrue."—*Post.*

OUR BISHOPS AND DEANS. By the Rev. F. ARNOLD, M.A. 2 vols. 8vo.. *(In the Press.)*

FROM THE THAMES TO THE TAMAR: A SUMMER ON THE SOUTH COAST. By the Rev. A. G. L'ESTRANGE. *Second Edition.* 8vo, with Illustrations. 15s.

"Mr. L'Estrange's pages have not the least flavour of the guide-book; they are pleasant and interesting chapters of local history, relieved by clear and unaffected descriptions of scenery, plainly written, yet picturesque and sufficient."—*Times.*

"To all who visit the south coast this book will afford much useful and interesting information."—*Standard.*

THE SWITZERS. By W. HEPWORTH DIXON. *Third Edition.* 1 vol. demy 8vo. 15s.

"Turn where we will there is the same impassioned eloquence, the same lavish wealth of metaphor, the same vigour of declamation, the same general glow upon the pages. Switzerland may be hackneyed as a country, yet there is freshness in Mr. Dixon's subjects. Mr. Dixon throws a passing glance at the snow peaks and glacier fields that are the Switzerland of the tourist. If he deals with the grand catastrophes of nature, with avalanche, flood, and storm, it is in their relation to the victims of the elements, for his topics are the people and their institutions. We assent entirely to the parable of his preface."—*Times.*

"A lively, interesting, and altogether novel book on Switzerland. It is full of valuable information on social, political, and ecclesiastical questions, and, like all Mr. Dixon's books, it is eminently readable."—*Daily News.*

"We advise every one who cares for good literature to get a copy of this brilliant, novel, and abundantly instructive account of the Switzers. The composition of the book is in the very best style."—*Morning Post.*

"A work of real and abiding value."—*Standard.*

MESSRS. HURST AND BLACKETT'S NEW WORKS—*Continued.*

MY RECOLLECTIONS, FROM 1806 to 1873.

By LORD WILLIAM PITT LENNOX. 2 vols. 8vo. 30s.

These volumes contain anecdotes and reminiscences of George IV., William IV. Louis XVIII., Prince Leopold, the Prince Consort, Prince Talleyrand, Napoleon III., the Empress Eugenie, the Prince Imperial, the Duke of Wellington, the Marquess of Anglesea, Lords Byron, Chesterfield, Brougham, Normanby, G. Bentinck, Dalling; Messrs. Pitt, Moore, Rogers, Hook, Barham, Dickens, Thackeray, Kean, Matthews, Young, Talma, Mdlle. Mars, Madame Malibran, &c.

"Lord William Lennox's book is a very good specimen of the class to which it belongs. In one way or another he has seen a great deal, and he records his experiences so as to amuse and interest his readers."—*Pall Mall Gazette.*

"It is impossible to find a more efficient chronicler of men and manners than the writer of these fascinating pages"—*John Bull.*

"A most entertaining work The author numbered among his friends and acquaintance all ranks of society—sovereigns, peers, statesmen, authors, wits, actors, and military men. He gives us some most delightful anecdotes and reminiscences."—*Court Journal.*

LIFE OF MOSCHELES; WITH SELECTIONS FROM HIS DIARIES AND CORRESPONDENCE.

By HIS WIFE. Adapted from the German by ARTHUR DUKE COLERIDGE. 2 vols. large post 8vo, with Portrait. 24s.

"This life of Moscheles will be a valuable book of reference for the musical historian, for the contents extend over a period of threescore years., commencing with 1794, and ending at 1870. We need scarcely state that all the portions of Moscheles' diary which refer to his intercourse with Beethoven, Hummel, Weber, Czerny, Spontini, Rossini, Auber, Halévy, Schumann, Cherubini, Spohr. Mendelssohn, F. David, Chopin, J B. Cramer. Clementi, John Field, Habeneck, Hauptmann, Kalkbrenner, Kiesewetter, C. Klingemann, Lablache, Dragonetti, Sontag, Persiani, Malibran, Paganini, Rachel, Ronzi de Begnis, De Beriot, Ernst, Donzelli, Cinti-Damoreau, Chelard, Bochsa, Laporte, Charles Kemble, Paton (Mrs. Wood), Schröder-Devrient, Mrs. Siddons, Sir H. Bishop, Sir G. Smart, Staudigl, Thalberg, Berlioz, Velluti, C. Young, Balfe, Braham, and many other artists of note in their time, will recall a flood of recollections. It was a delicate task for Madame Moscheles to select from the diaries in reference to living persons, but her extracts have been judiciously made. Moscheles writes fairly of what is called the 'Music of the Future' and its disciples, and his judgments on Herr Wagner, Dr. Liszt, Rubenstein, Dr. von Bülow, Litolff, &c., whether as composers or executants, are in a liberal spirit. He recognizes cheerfully the talents of our native artists, Sir Sterndale Bennett, Mr. Macfarren, Madame Arabella Goddard, Mr. John Barnett, Mr. Hullah, Mrs. Shaw, Mr. A. Sullivan, &c. The celebrities with whom Moscheles came in contact, include Sir Walter Scott, Sir Robert Peel, the late Duke of Cambridge, the Bunsens, Louis Philippe, Napoleon the Third, Humboldt, Henry Heine, Thomas More, Count Nesselrode, the Duchess of Orleans, Prof. Wolf, &c. Indeed, the two volumes are full of amusing anecdotes."—*Athenæum.*

"The publication of these memoirs will give satisfaction to many of our readers. The devotees of music in this country are both numerous and earnest. By this class these volumes will be hailed with particular delight; but they will be acceptable also to a far wider circle—to all who enjoy a sonata at home or a symphony in the concert-room. The scope of the work gives it this popular interest, apart from the technical value it possess. It is as well 'a record of the life of Moscheles' as 'a chronicle of the musical history of his time'—a period of sixty years."—*Times.*

"This work is full of interesting information and pleasant gossip about the musical events of the last half-century. Moscheles kept up to the day of his death a diary, in which he recorded all his experiences, and his constant intercourse with such men as Beethoven, Weber, Mendelssohn, and Schumann, enabled him to collect a mass of facts and anecdotes which throw much valuable light on recent musical history. The greater part of the diary was written in London, where Moscheles settled in 1826; and he describes in a vivid and attractive style the various incidents of his career in England, and the events which most interested our musical public during that time. Of all Moscheles' recollectious none are so interesting as those of Mendelssohn."—*Pall Mall Gazette.*

MESSRS. HURST AND BLACKETT'S NEW WORKS—*Continued.*

VOLS. I. & II. OF HER MAJESTY'S TOWER.

By W. HEPWORTH DIXON. DEDICATED BY EXPRESS PERMISSION TO THE QUEEN. *Sixth Edition.* 8vo. 30s.

CONTENTS:—The Pile—Inner Ward and Outer Ward—The Wharf—River Rights—The White Tower—Charles of Orleans—Uncle Gloucester—Prison Rules—Beauchamp Tower—The good Lord Cobham—King and Cardinal—The Pilgrimage of Grace—Madge Cheyne—Heirs to the Crown—The Nine Days' Queen—Dethroned—The Men of Kent—Courtney—No Cross no Crown—Cranmer, Latimer, Ridley—White Roses—Princess Margaret—Plot and Counterplot—Monsieur Charles—Bishop of Ross—Murder of Northumberland—Philip the Confessor—Mass in the Tower—Sir Walter Raleigh—The Arabella Plot—Raleigh's Walk—The Villain Waad—The Garden House—The Brick Tower—The Anglo-Spanish Plot—Factions at Court—Lord Grey of Wilton—Old English Catholics—The English Jesuits—White Webbs—The Priests' Plot—Wilton Court—Last of a Noble Line—Powder-Plot Room—Guy Fawkes—Origin of the Plot—Vinegar House—Conspiracy at Large—The Jesuit's Move—In London—November, 1605—Hunted Down—In the Tower—Search for Garnet—End of the English Jesuits—The Catholic Lords—Harry Percy—The Wizard Earl—A Real Arabella Plot—William Seymour—The Escape—Pursuit—Dead in the Tower—Lady Frances Howard—Robert Carr—Powder Poisoning

---

FROM THE TIMES:—"All the civilized world—English, Continental, and American—takes an interest in the Tower of London. The Tower is the stage upon which has been enacted some of the grandest dramas and saddest tragedies in our national annals. If, in imagination, we take our stand on those time-worn walls, and let century after century flit past us, we shall see in due succession the majority of the most famous men and lovely women of England in the olden time. We shall see them jesting, jousting, love-making, plotting, and then anon, perhaps, commending their souls to God in the presence of a hideous masked figure, bearing an axe in his hands. It is such pictures as these that Mr. Dixon, with considerable skill as an historical limner, has set before us in these volumes. Mr. Dixon dashes off the scenes of Tower history with great spirit. His descriptions are given with such terseness and vigour that we should spoil them by any attempt at condensation. As favourable examples of his narrative powers we may call attention to the story of the beautiful but unpopular Elinor, Queen of Henry III., and the description of Anne Boleyn's first and second arrivals at the Tower. Then we have the story of the bold Bishop of Durham, who escapes by the aid of a cord hidden in a wine-jar; and the tale of Maud Fitzwalter, imprisoned and murdered by the caitiff John. Passing onwards, we meet Charles of Orleans, the poetic French Prince, captured at Agincourt, and detained for five-and-twenty years a prisoner in the Tower. Next we encounter the baleful form of Richard of Gloucester, and are filled with indignation at the blackest of the black Tower deeds. As we draw nearer to modern times, we have the sorrowful story of the Nine Days' Queen, poor little Lady Jane Grey. The chapter entitled "No Cross, no Crown" is one of the most affecting in the book. A mature man can scarcely read it without feeling the tears ready to trickle from his eyes. No part of the first volume yields in interest to the chapters which are devoted to the story of Sir Walter Raleigh. The greater part of the second volume is occupied with the story of the Gunpowder Plot. The narrative is extremely interesting, and will repay perusal. Another *cause celèbre* possessed of a perennial interest, is the murder of Sir Thomas Overbury by Lord and Lady Somerset. Mr. Dixon tells the tale skilfully. In conclusion, we may congratulate the author on this work. Both volumes are decidedly attractive, and throw much light on our national history."

"From first to last this work overflows with new information and original thought, with poetry and picture. In these fascinating pages Mr. Dixon discharges alternately the functions of the historian, and the historic biographer, with the insight, art, humour and accurate knowledge which never fail him when he undertakes to illumine the darksome recesses of our national story."—*Morning Post.*

"We earnestly recommend this remarkable work to those in quest of amusement and instruction, at once solid and refined.."—*Daily Telegraph.*

MESSRS. HURST AND BLACKETT'S NEW WORKS—*Continued.*

VOLS. III. & IV. OF HER MAJESTY'S TOWER.

By W. HEPWORTH DIXON. DEDICATED BY EXPRESS PERMISSION TO THE QUEEN. Completing the Work. *Third Edition.* Demy 8vo. 30s.

CONTENTS:—A Favourite; A Favourite's Friend; The Countess of Suffolk; To the Tower; Lady Catherine Manners; House of Villiers; Revolution; Fall of Lord Bacon; A Spanish Match; Spaniolizing; Henry De Vere; The Matter of Holland; Sea Affairs; The Pirate War; Port and Court; A New Romanzo; Move and Counter-move; Pirate and Prison; In the Marshalsea; The Spanish Olive; Prisons Opened; A Parliament; Digby, Earl of Bristol; Turn of Fortune; Eliot Eloquent; Felton's Knife; An Assassin; Nine Gentlemen in the Tower; A King's Revenge; Charles I.; Pillars of State and Church; End of Wentworth; Laud's Last Troubles; The Lieutenant's House; A Political Romance; Philosophy at Bay; Fate of an Idealist; Britannia; Killing not Murder; A Second Buckingham; Roger, Earl of Castlemaine; A Life of Plots; The Two Penns; A Quaker's Cell; Colonel Blood; Crown Jewels, King and Colonel; Rye House Plot; Murder; A Patriot; The Good Old Cause; James, Duke of Monmouth; The Unjust Judge; The Scottish Lords; The Countess of Nithisdale; Escaped, Cause of the Pretender; Reformers and Reform, Reform Riots; Sir Francis Burdett; A Summons to the Tower; Arthur Thistlewood; A Cabinet Council; Cato Street; Pursuit; Last Prisoners in the Tower.

"Mr. Dixon's lively and accurate work."—*Times.*

"This book is thoroughly entertaining, well-written, and instructive."—*Examiner.*

"These volumes will place Mr. Dixon permanently on the roll of English authors who have rendered their country a service, by his putting on record a truthful and brilliant account of that most popular and instructive relic of antiquity. 'Her Majesty's Tower;' the annals of which, as related in these volumes, are by turns exciting and amusing, while they never fail to interest. Our ancient stronghold could have had no better historian than Mr. Dixon."—*Post.*

"By his merits of literary execution, his vivacious portraitures of historical figures, his masterly powers of narrative and description, and the force and graceful ease of his style, Mr. Dixon will keep his hold upon a multitude of readers."—*Illustrated News.*

"These volumes are two galleries of richly painted portraits of the noblest men and most brilliant women, besides others commemorated by English history. The grand old Royal Keep, palace and prison by turns, is revivified in these volumes, which close the narrative, extending from the era of Sir John Eliot, who saw Raleigh die in Palace Yard, to that of Thistlewood, the last prisoner immured in the Tower. Few works are given to us, in these days, so abundant in originality and research as Mr. Dixon's."—*Standard.*

HISTORY OF WILLIAM PENN, Founder of

Pennsylvania. By W. HEPWORTH DIXON. A NEW LIBRARY EDITION. 1 vol. demy 8vo, with Portrait. 12s.

"Mr. Dixon's 'William Penn' is, perhaps, the best of his books. He has now revised and issued it with the addition of much fresh matter. It is now offered in a sumptuous volume, matching with Mr. Dixon's recent books, to a new generation of readers, who will thank Mr. Dixon for his interesting and instructive memoir of one of the worthies of England."—*Examiner.*

"'William Penn' is a fine and noble work. Eloquent, picturesque, and epigramatic in style, subtle and philosophical in insight, and moderate and accurate in statement, it is a model of what a biography ought to be."—*Sunday Times.*

"The character of this great Christian Englishman, William Penn, a true hero of moral and civil conquests, is one of the fairest in modern history, and may be studied with profit by his countrymen of all ages. This biography of him now finally put into shape as a standard work of its kind, is Mr. Dixon's most useful production. Few books have a more genial and wholesome interest, or convey more beneficial instruction."—*Illustrated News.*

MESSRS. HURST AND BLACKETT'S NEW WORKS—*Continued.*

CRISS-CROSS JOURNEYS. By Walter Thornbury. 2 vols. crown 8vo. 21s.

"A lively, graphic, and interesting book."—*Daily News.*

"An interesting book. Very pleasant companions are Mr. Thornbury's two volumes of travel, revealing as they do glimpses of the oldest and newest world, enlivened with countless anecdotes and many personal adventures. The reader will find Mr. Thornbury a fascinating *raconteur.*"—*Graphic.*

"Mr. Thornbury is a shrewd and observant traveller. His descriptions are singularly life-like and truthful, and his humour is genuine. His journeys are excellent. His descriptions of America are both truthful and valuable, and what he says about Egypt and Russia is worth saying and well said."—*Sunday Times.*

BRIDES AND BRIDALS. By J. C. Jeaffreson, B.A., Oxon. *Second Edition.* 2 vols. 8vo. 30s.

"In this book Mr. Jeaffreson appeals to an audience even larger than those addressed in his books about Lawyers, Doctors, and the Clergy. His 'Brides and Bridals' cannot fail to go straight to the heart of every woman in England. We doubt not that these volumes will be carefully scanned by fair eyes of all ages and conditions, and will afford no less amusement than instruction."—*Athenæum.*

THE LITERARY LIFE OF THE REV. WILLIAM HARNESS, Vicar of All Saints, Knightsbridge, and Prebendary of St. Paul's. By the Rev. A. G. L'Estrange. 8vo. 15s.

"The book is a pleasant book, and will be found excellent reading. All those to whom the good name of Byron is dear, will read with an almost exquisite pleasure the testimony given by Harness."—*Athenæum.*

LIFE AND LETTERS OF WILLIAM BEWICK, THE ARTIST. Edited by Thomas Landseer, A.R.A. 2 vols.

"Bewick's fellow pupil and old friend, Mr. T. Landseer, the famous engraver, has put the materials before us together with much skill. The literary sketches which Bewick made of Hazlitt, Haydon, Shelley, Keats, Scott, Hogg, Jeffrey, Maturin, and others, are extremely bright, apt, and clear."—*Athenæum.*

THE LION AND THE ELEPHANT. By the late C. J. Andersson, Author of "Lake Ngami," &c. Edited by L. Lloyd, author of "Field Sports of the North," &c. 8vo. With Illustrations. 15s.

"This handsome volume contains a most graphic account of the adventures of Mr. Andersson, from papers which he left behind him, and which have been most ably edited by Mr. Lloyd. The favourite pursuit of the deceased traveller was the chase of the lion, and he gives us most minute particulars of the habits and customs of the royal beast. The portion of the work anent elephants is of equal interest. All fond of tales of adventure and daring should procure this capital book."—*John Bull.*

"This book is pleasant reading. It gives much valuable information, and many excellent stories about these interesting animals."—*Examiner.*

"Interesting to the general reader, this attractive book will be found especially worthy of the attention of naturalists and sportsmen."—*Standard.*

"An attractive and exciting volume, full of adventures and hair-breadth escapes, and which will be read with interest and delight."—*Graphic.*

MODERN TURKEY. By J. Lewis Farley, Consul of the Sublime Porte at Bristol. *Second Edition.* 1 vol. 14s.

"Mr. Farley has a good deal of interesting information to communicate in regard to the resources of modern Turkey; and we may add that he puts it briefly, clearly, and in an agreeable style."—*Saturday Review.*

MESSRS. HURST AND BLACKETT'S NEW WORKS—*Continued.*

TO AND FROM CONSTANTINOPLE. By HUBERT E. H. JERNINGHAM. 8vo, with Illustrations. 15s.

"Mr. Jerningham has filled a very agreeable volume with the tale of his excursions during the last three years among scenes of classic or Oriental interest. His style is lively, clear, and picturesque."—*Saturday Review.*

"Mr. Jerningham's work includes trips from Brindisi to Athens, to Corinth by Nauplia, and Mycenæ, to Mount Athos, to Cyzicus, Broussa, Nicomedia, and Nicæa, besides chapters upon Constantinople and its environs. While the most interesting parts of the work to a general reader are the descriptions of the people, the author gives a mass of notices as to the antiquities and interesting sites of the localities he visits."—*Standard.*

THE LUSHAI EXPEDITION. 1871-72. By R. G. WOODTHORPE, Lieut. R.E. 1 vol. demy 8vo, with Illustrations. 15s.

"Lieut. Woodthorpe's account of the Lushai Expedition is important as well as interesting. The writer excels in description, and is very pleasing in his geographical and scenic sketches."—*Post.*

FREE RUSSIA. By W. HEPWORTH DIXON. *Third Edition.* 2 vols. 8vo, with Coloured Illustrations. 30s.

"Mr. Dixon's book will be certain not only to interest but to please its readers and it deserves to do so. It contains a great deal that is worthy of attention, and is likely to produce a very useful effect. The ignorance of the English people with respect to Russia has long been so dense that we cannot avoid being grateful to a writer who has taken the trouble to make personal acquaintance with that seldom-visited land, and to bring before the eyes of his countrymen a picture of its scenery and its people, which is so novel and interesting that it can scarcely fail to arrest their attention."—*Saturday Review.*

TURKISH HAREMS & CIRCASSIAN HOMES. By MRS. HARVEY, of Ickwell Bury. 8vo. *Second Edition.* 15s.

"Mrs. Harvey not only saw a great deal, but saw all that she did see to the best advantage. In noticing the intrinsic interest of Mrs. Harvey's book, we must not forget to say a word for her ability as a writer."—*Times.*

MEMOIRS OF QUEEN HORTENSE, MOTHER OF NAPOLEON III. Cheaper Edition, in 1 vol. 6s.

"A biography of the beautiful and unhappy Queen, more satisfactory than any we have yet met with."—*Daily News.*

THE CITIES OF THE NATIONS FELL. By the Rev. JOHN CUMMING, D.D. *Second Edition.* 1 vol. 6s.

"The work before us contains much historical information of interest and value. We must applaud here, as we applauded in his treatise on The Seventh Vial, the skill and diligence of the author in the vast and careful selection of facts, both physical and moral, the interest of each when taken singly, and the striking picture of the whole when presented collectively to the view."—*Record.*

THE EXILES AT ST. GERMAINS. By the Author of "The Ladye Shakerley." 1 vol. 7s. 6d. bound.

"The whole narrative is picturesque, graphic, and entertaining, as well as moral and pathetic."—*Morning Post.*

"'The Exiles at St. Germains' is an excellent attempt to depict the life of the latter Stuarts while they lived under the protection of the Lilies of France. The author is that skilled penwoman who wrote 'The Ladye Shakerley,' and she has seized fully the spirit of the Stuart age. 'The Exiles at St. Germains' will be every whit as popular as 'The Ladye Shakerley.'"—*Standard.*

THE NEW AND POPULAR NOVELS.

PUBLISHED BY HURST & BLACKETT.

ROUGH HEWN. By Mrs. DAY, Author of "From Birth to Bridal," &c. 3 vols.

"In many respects an excellent novel."—*Athenæum.*

"A novel good to read and pleasant to remember."—*Spectator.*

"'Rough Hewn' is a more carefully-constructed novel than we have read for some time. It is a refreshing, healthy, and interesting story. The characters are natural and well drawn. Mrs. Day's novel excels not only in the thoroughly unaffected simplicity of its style, but also in being the composition of an educated and cultivated woman."—*Examiner.*

FOR LOVE AND LIFE. By MRS. OLIPHANT, Author of "Chronicles of Carlingford," "May," "Ombra," &c. 3 v.

"'For Love and Life' is equal in all respects to the reputation of its writer. It will be read with delight."—*John Bull.*

"This novel is well worth reading. The story is interesting, the plot is original, and every character is a study."—*Daily News.*

"'For Love and Life' may be classed among those works of Mrs. Oliphant which are likely to be the most popular. Every piece of portraiture is good and true, and a vein of bright humour runs through the whole."—*Graphic.*

OUT OF COURT. By Mrs. CASHEL HOEY, Author of "A Golden Sorrow," &c. 3 vols.

"A capital novel, which it is delightful to read, and which it will be pleasant to remember. It is emphatically what Charles Lamb would have called a healthy book."—*Pall Mall Gazette.*

"This story is one of very considerable power and of a noble aim. There are frequent touches of humour in it, and the pathos is deep and unaffected."—*Spectator.*

"A most fascinating and admirably constructed story. It is as powerful as it is well written and well imagined."—*Post.*

SECOND-COUSIN SARAH. By F. W. ROBINSON, Author of "Grandmother's Money," "No Church," &c. 3 vols.

"A readable story. It has plenty of incident."—*Athenæum.*

"A book which it is impossible to lay aside. The writer exercises a marvellous fascination over the reader, from his life-like delineations of character, and the magical power of the conversations."—*John Bull.*

THE BLUE RIBBON. By the Author of "St. Olave's," "Janita's Cross," &c. 3 vols.

"An interesting story. We like 'The Blue Ribbon' very much.'—*Spectator.*

"An admirable story. The character of the heroine is original and skilfully worked out, and an interest is cast around her which never flags. The sketches of society in a cathedral city are very vivid and amusing."—*Post.*

BROKEN BONDS. By HAWLEY SMART, Author of "Breezie Langton," "False Cards," &c. 3 vols.

"'Broken Bonds' will thoroughly satisfy all lovers of stories of adventure. Its incidents are ingeniously invented, and described with spirit."—*Pall Mall Gazette.*

COLONEL DACRE. By the Author of "Caste." 3 v.

"There is much that is attractive both in Colonel Dacre and the simple-hearted girl whom he honours with his love."—*Athenæum.*

NATHANIEL VAUGHAN: PRIEST AND MAN.

Under the Especial Patronage of Her Majesty.

Published annually, in One Vol., royal 8vo, with the Arms beautifully engraved, handsomely bound, with gilt edges, price **31s. 6d.**

LODGE'S PEERAGE
AND BARONETAGE,
CORRECTED BY THE NOBILITY.

THE FORTY-THIRD EDITION FOR 1874 IS NOW READY.

Lodge's Peerage and Baronetage is acknowledged to be the most complete, as well as the most elegant, work of the kind. As an established and authentic authority on all questions respecting the family histories, honours, and connections of the titled aristocracy, no work has ever stood so high. It is published under the especial patronage of Her Majesty, and is annually corrected throughout, from the personal communications of the Nobility. It is the only work of its class in which, *the type being kept constantly standing*, every correction is made in its proper place to the date of publication, an advantage which gives it supremacy over all its competitors. Independently of its full and authentic information respecting the existing Peers and Baronets of the realm, the most sedulous attention is given in its pages to the collateral branches of the various noble families, and the names of many thousand individuals are introduced, which do not appear in other records of the titled classes. For its authority, correctness, and facility of arrangement, and the beauty of its typography and binding, the work is justly entitled to the place it occupies on the tables of Her Majesty and the Nobility.

LIST OF THE PRINCIPAL CONTENTS.

- Historical View of the Peerage.
- Parliamentary Roll of the House of Lords.
- English, Scotch, and Irish Peers, in their orders of Precedence.
- Alphabetical List of Peers of Great Britain and the United Kingdom, holding superior rank in the Scotch or Irish Peerage.
- Alphabetical list of Scotch and Irish Peers, holding superior titles in the Peerage of Great Britain and the United Kingdom.
- A Collective list of Peers, in their order of Precedence.
- Table of Precedency among Men.
- Table of Precedency among Women.
- The Queen and the Royal Family.
- Peers of the Blood Royal.
- The Peerage, alphabetically arranged.
- Families of such Extinct Peers as have left Widows or Issue.
- Alphabetical List of the Surnames of all the Peers.
- The Archbishops and Bishops of England, Ireland, and the Colonies.
- The Baronetage alphabetically arranged.
- Alphabetical List of Surnames assumed by members of Noble Families.
- Alphabetical List of the Second Titles of Peers, usually borne by their Eldest Sons.
- Alphabetical Index to the Daughters of Dukes, Marquises, and Earls, who, having married Commoners, retain the title of Lady before their own Christian and their Husband's Surnames.
- Alphabetical Index to the Daughters of Viscounts and Barons, who, having married Commoners, are styled Honourable Mrs.; and, in case of the husband being a Baronet or Knight, Honourable Lady.
- Mottoes alphabetically arranged and translated.

"A work which corrects all errors of former works. It is a most useful publication. We are happy to bear testimony to the fact that scrupulous accuracy is a distinguishing feature of this book."—*Times.*

"Lodge's Peerage must supersede all other works of the kind, for two reasons: first, it is on a better plan; and secondly, it is better executed. We can safely pronounce it to be the readiest, the most useful, and exactest of modern works on the subject."—*Spectator.*

"A work of great value. It is the most faithful record we possess of the aristocracy of the day."—*Post.*

"The best existing and we believe the best possible Peerage. It is the standard

HURST & BLACKETT'S STANDARD LIBRARY
(CONTINUED.)

VIII.—CARDINAL WISEMAN'S RECOLLECTIONS OF THE LAST FOUR POPES.

"A picturesque book on Rome and its ecclesiastical sovereigns, by an eloquent Roman Catholic. Cardinal Wiseman has treated a special subject with so much geniality, that his recollections will excite no ill-feeling in those who are most conscientiously opposed to every idea of human infallibility represented in Papal domination."—*Athenæum.*

IX.—A LIFE FOR A LIFE.

BY THE AUTHOR OF "JOHN HALIFAX, GENTLEMAN."

"In 'A Life for a Life' the author is fortunate in a good subject, and has produced a work of strong effect."—*Athenæum.*

X.—THE OLD COURT SUBURB. By LEIGH HUNT.

"A delightful book, that will be welcome to all readers, and most welcome to those who have a love for the best kinds of reading."—*Examiner.*

"A more agreeable and entertaining book has not been published since Boswell produced his reminiscences of Johnson."—*Observer.*

XI.—MARGARET AND HER BRIDESMAIDS.

"We recommend all who are in search of a fascinating novel to read this work for themselves. They will find it well worth their while. There are a freshness and originality about it quite charming."—*Athenæum.*

XII.—THE OLD JUDGE. By SAM SLICK.

"The publications included in this Library have all been of good quality; many give information while they entertain, and of that class the book before us is a specimen. The manner in which the Cheap Editions forming the series is produced, deserves especial mention. The paper and print are unexceptionable; there is a steel engraving in each volume, and the outsides of them will satisfy the purchaser who likes to see books in handsome uniform."—*Examiner.*

XIII.—DARIEN. By ELIOT WARBURTON.

"This last production of the author of 'The Crescent and the Cross' has the same elements of a very wide popularity. It will please its thousands."—*Globe.*

XIV.—FAMILY ROMANCE; OR, DOMESTIC ANNALS OF THE ARISTOCRACY.

BY SIR BERNARD BURKE, ULSTER KING OF ARMS.

"It were impossible to praise too highly this most interesting book. It ought to be found on every drawing-room table."—*Standard.*

XV.—THE LAIRD OF NORLAW. By MRS. OLIPHANT.

"The 'Laird of Norlaw' fully sustains the author's high reputation."—*Sunday Times.*

XVI.—THE ENGLISHWOMAN IN ITALY.

"We can praise Mrs. Gretton's book as interesting, unexaggerated, and full of opportune instruction."—*Times.*

XVII.—NOTHING NEW.

BY THE AUTHOR OF "JOHN HALIFAX, GENTLEMAN."

"'Nothing New' displays all those superior merits which have made 'John Halifax one of the most popular works of the day."—*Post.*

XVIII.—FREER'S LIFE OF JEANNE D'ALBRET.

"Nothing can be more interesting than Miss Freer's story of the life of Jeanne D'Albret, and the narrative is as trustworthy as it is attractive."—*Post.*

XIX.—THE VALLEY OF A HUNDRED FIRES.

BY THE AUTHOR OF "MARGARET AND HER BRIDESMAIDS."

"If asked to classify this work, we should give it a place between 'John Halifax' and 'The Caxtons.'"—*Standard.*

XX.—THE ROMANCE OF THE FORUM.

BY PETER BURKE, SERGEANT AT LAW.

"A work of singular interest, which can never fail to charm. The present cheap and elegant edition includes the true story of the Colleen Bawn."—*Illustrated News.*

XXI.—ADELE. By JULIA KAVANAGH.

"'Adele' is the best work we have read by Miss Kavanagh; it is a charming story full of delicate character-painting."—*Athenæum.*

XXII.—STUDIES FROM LIFE.

BY THE AUTHOR OF "JOHN HALIFAX, GENTLEMAN."

"These 'Studies from Life' are remarkable for graphic power and observation. The book will not diminish the reputation of the accomplished author."—*Saturday Review.*

XXIII.—GRANDMOTHER'S MONEY.

"We commend 'Grandmother's Money' to readers in search of a good novel. The characters are true to human nature, and the story is interesting."—*Athenæum.*

XXIV.—A BOOK ABOUT DOCTORS.

BY J. C. JEAFFRESON.

"A delightful book."—*Athenæum.* "A book to be read and re-read; fit for the study as well as the drawing-room table and the circulating library."—*Lancet.*

XXV.—NO CHURCH.

"We advise all who have the opportunity to read this book."—*Athenæum.*

XXVI.—MISTRESS AND MAID.

BY THE AUTHOR OF "JOHN HALIFAX, GENTLEMAN."

"A good wholesome book, gracefully written, and as pleasant to read as it is instructive."—*Athenæum.* "A charming tale charmingly told."—*Standard.*

XXVII.—LOST AND SAVED. By HON. MRS. NORTON.

"'Lost and Saved' will be read with eager interest. It is a vigorous novel."—*Times.* "A novel of rare excellence. It is Mrs. Norton's best prose work."—*Examiner.*

XXVIII.—LES MISERABLES. By VICTOR HUGO.

AUTHORISED COPYRIGHT ENGLISH TRANSLATION.

"The merits of 'Les Miserables' do not merely consist in the conception of it as a whole; it abounds with details of unequalled beauty. M. Victor Hugo has stamped upon every page the hall-mark of genius."—*Quarterly Review.*

XXIX.—BARBARA'S HISTORY.

BY AMELIA B. EDWARDS.

"It is not often that we light upon a novel of so much merit and interest as 'Barbara's History.' It is a work conspicuous for taste and literary culture. It is a very graceful and charming book, with a well-managed story, clearly-cut characters, and sentiments expressed with an exquisite elocution. It is a book which the world will like."—*Times.*

XXX.—LIFE OF THE REV. EDWARD IRVING.

BY MRS. OLIPHANT.

"A good book on a most interesting theme."—*Times.*

"A truly interesting and most affecting memoir. Irving's Life ought to have a niche in every gallery of religious biography. There are few lives that will be fuller of instruction, interest, and consolation."—*Saturday Review.*

XXXI.—ST. OLAVE'S.

"This charming novel is the work of one who possesses a great talent for writing, as well as experience and knowledge of the world."—*Athenæum.*

XXXII.—SAM SLICK'S AMERICAN HUMOUR.

"Dip where you will into this lottery of fun, you are sure to draw out a prize."—*Post.*

HURST & BLACKETT'S STANDARD LIBRARY

XXXIII.—CHRISTIAN'S MISTAKE.

BY THE AUTHOR OF "JOHN HALIFAX, GENTLEMAN."

"A more charming story, to our taste, has rarely been written. The writer has hit off a circle of varied characters all true to nature. Even if tried by the standard of the Archbishop of York, we should expect that even he would pronounce 'Christian's Mistake' a novel without a fault."—*Times.*

XXXIV.—ALEC FORBES OF HOWGLEN.

BY GEORGE MAC DONALD, LL.D.

"No account of this story would give any idea of the profound interest that pervades the work from the first page to the last."—*Athenæum.*

XXXV.—AGNES. By MRS. OLIPHANT.

"'Agnes' is a novel superior to any of Mrs. Oliphant's former works."—*Athenæum.*
"A story whose pathetic beauty will appeal irresistibly to all readers."—*Post.*

XXXVI.—A NOBLE LIFE.

BY THE AUTHOR OF "JOHN HALIFAX, GENTLEMAN."

"This is one of those pleasant tales in which the author of 'John Halifax' speaks out of a generous heart the purest truths of life."—*Examiner.*

XXXVII.—NEW AMERICA. By HEPWORTH DIXON.

"A very interesting book. Mr. Dixon has written thoughtfully and well."—*Times.*
Mr. Dixon's very entertaining and instructive work on New America."—*Pall Mall Gaz.*
"We recommend every one who feels any interest in human nature to read Mr. Dixon's very interesting book."—*Saturday Review.*

XXXVIII.—ROBERT FALCONER.

BY GEORGE MAC DONALD, LL.D.

"'Robert Falconer' is a work brimful of life and humour and of the deepest human interest. It is a book to be returned to again and again for the deep and searching knowledge it evinces of human thoughts and feelings."—*Athenæum.*

XXXIX.—THE WOMAN'S KINGDOM.

BY THE AUTHOR OF "JOHN HALIFAX, GENTLEMAN."

"'The Woman's Kingdom' sustains the author's reputation as a writer of the purest and noblest kind of domestic stories.—*Athenæum.*

XL.—ANNALS OF AN EVENTFUL LIFE.

BY GEORGE WEBBE DASENT, D.C.L.

"A racy, well-written, and original novel. The interest never flags. The whole work sparkles with wit and humour."—*Quarterly Review.*

XLI.—DAVID ELGINBROD.

BY GEORGE MAC DONALD, LL.D.

"A novel which is the work of a man of true genius. It will attract the highest class of readers."—*Times.*

XLII.—A BRAVE LADY.

BY THE AUTHOR OF "JOHN HALIFAX, GENTLEMAN."

"A very good novel; a thoughtful, well-written book, showing a tender sympathy with human nature, and permeated by a pure and noble spirit."—*Examiner.*

XLIII.—HANNAH.

BY THE AUTHOR OF "JOHN HALIFAX, GENTLEMAN."

"A powerful novel of social and domestic life. One of the most successful efforts of a successful novelist."—*Daily News.*
'A very pleasant, healthy story, well and artistically told. The book is sure of a wide circle of readers. The character of Hannah is one of rare beauty."—*Standard.*

XLIV.—SAM SLICK'S AMERICANS AT HOME.